Defusing the Family Business Time Bomb

JENIFER BARTMAN & EVELYN JACKS

Published by Knowledge Bureau

KNOWLEDGE BUREAU
NEWSBOOKS

WINNIPEG, MANITOBA, CANADA

ISBN 978-1-77297-065-4

Printed and bound in Canada

Canadian Cataloguing in Publication Data

1.   Business – Canada – Popular works. 2. Personal Financial Planning – Canada – Popular works. 3. Tax - Canada

I.   Title. Defusing the Family Business Time Bomb

HG179.R683 2005   332.024'01   C2009-900948-X

Published by: Knowledge Bureau, Inc.

187 St. Mary's Road, Winnipeg, Manitoba R2H 1J2

Tel: (204) 953-4769 Email: reception@knowledgebureau.com

Research and Editorial Assistance: Nancy Folliott

Cover and Page Design: Bruce Reimer, Reimer Communications

This book dedicated to family.

Despite our complex lives in a constantly changing world,
our families give us foundational roots, the confidence to
take flight, and at the core, relationships to build memories
future generations will want to share.

Our opportunity is to make those memories powerful and
inspirational.

Here's to our families, roots and wings!

Acknowledgements:

We would like to sincerely thank Bruce Reimer, Nancy Folliott, Walter Harder and Larry Frostiak for all their help in making the ideas in this book come alive.

Contents

INTRODUCTION
Defusing the Family Business Time Bomb

Kaboom! That's the familiar sound of another day in many family businesses.

Siblings are squabbling, spouse is stressed.

Staff members need direction.

Customer demands are increasing.

Technology is struggling to keep up.

Financial information is swirling, but yet, doesn't shed much light on why results are not what was expected... again.

Competitive pressures are rising, with new products, services, advertising, and locations. This would be something to investigate further, if only there was time...

Plans are revisited, only to be dismissed again; a constant state of flux, where little is resolved....

Founders are growing older and there is uncertainty as to what the future holds. Will they stay? Will they go?

Will the next generation get a chance to lead the business or will they decide to travel a different path?

Pain points. Every business has them. In fact, at least some of these issues may very well be a part of **your** reality every day.

More than ever in recent history, the family business is under siege from a diverse set of disruptions and risks: demographic changes, rapidly emerging technologies, political and economic factors, and new and complex tax rules that threaten the investment in the family business and its transition to the next generation. *Business leaders are, in fact, facing the most explosive changes on every one of these fronts in more than a generation.*

While these are all important issues for all Canadians; they are especially pertinent to small to medium-sized businesses, which make up a significant portion of Canada's business community and account for a large portion of the economic activity in this country.[1] In fact, small businesses account for 97.9 percent of all firms in Canada and these companies create

---

1 According to Stats Canada (2015): As of December 2015, there were 1.17 million employer businesses in Canada; of these, 1.14 million (97.9 percent) businesses were small businesses (1 to 99 employees); 21,415 (1.8 percent) were medium-sized businesses (100 to 499 employees); and 2,933 (0.3 percent) were large enterprises (over 500) employees).

close to 90% of all new jobs in Canada and employee millions of people every year.

Here's the key issue: the continued health of the small business community matters. *When family businesses are at risk, the financial future of their owners, relatives, future successors, employees, and community could also be in peril.*

The current environment demands a lens on the issues facing family businesses—one with a much wider focus—to bring what's happening on the outside into the picture. The stakes are much higher today than simply thinking about people, processes, and planning at a business level; rather, a much more strategic, holistic, and broader perspective is required by all stakeholders of the company as our economy faces new headwinds.

To put this in context, here's a look at the threats that are brewing and aligning in the external environment, impacting the business world as a whole, with particular implications for family enterprises.

Demographic factors. Research has consistently shown that the vast majority of business leaders have not taken tangible steps to formally prepare for succession of their companies, be it to family members or other parties. This is especially true of businesses owned and run by those in the "Baby Boom" generation, but also relates to companies with even older leadership. Key steps in a successful transition include having a written succession plan, identifying a qualified successor, determining a firm timeline for transition, and establishing the basic terms of the transaction, such as valuation, payment structure, and financing requirements.

But, in many cases, business leaders have little more than an "idea in their head" or expectation that their "kids will take over the company", which is well short of what is required to affect a succession transaction. In fact, there are many companies with leadership of an advanced age, where transition should have occurred years ago. When considered in numbers, this is significant to the economy as a whole, given the growing number of entities that will lack leadership (and ownership) over the next short while.

At the same time, the next generation of potential business leaders has been met with limited advancement opportunity, with the reasons ranging from a lack of turnover at the leadership level, to the challenges associated with securing the necessary capital to fund a transaction. Couple this with a relatively limited number of potential successors and it is evident that the road to future sustainability for many companies is littered with minefields.

These new economy risks magnify the typical problems that family businesses face, given that most owner/managers do not start the succession planning process early enough, leaving plenty of questions yet to be answered:

- Will the family business survive the transition to the next generation?

- How will the founders fund their retirement and receive a return on their investment?

- How will the next generation of business leaders cope with the multifaceted challenge of taking the company forward into the future—into a world characterized by rapid change, market volatility, shrinking profit margins, increased regulatory requirements, public scrutiny, and the rising presence of environmental issues?

The difficulty in addressing these issues and many others can result in succession related efforts grinding to a halt; one that could last for years, which only reinforces the problem.

Disruption of key industries. It is no secret that a proliferation of technological and scientific advancements has been occurring for decades, however, this process has accelerated during the past several years, bringing with it changes in market expectations, new competitive forces, and a higher level of sophistication that many companies struggle to address. This rapid and ongoing digital and technological advancement has the potential to make the companies of yesterday, those that have not kept pace with evolution, less relevant, thereby reducing their worth and making transition to new ownership less likely.

This does not only apply to companies that would be regarded as definitively archaic, but rather, it impacts many entities that have fallen even *slightly* behind the times. Why is this the case? Because there are typically other competitive offerings that have not only maintained pace, but have exceeded it, putting them in a much stronger position in the marketplace. In comparison, the costs associated with bringing a weaker entity to a more contemporary level might simply not be worth the effort.

For many business leaders, these circumstances represent a compelling and sobering fact, one that is often discovered too late. In the event of not being able to transition their company for these reasons, they continue to operate, until there is no basis left for doing so, and sadly, no saleable equity in the business.

Dramatic change in the global economy. As countries evolve, alliances shift, and trade policies become more uncertain, it can be very difficult for companies to have a sense of where they stand in what has become an unfamiliar world. With a lack of clarity comes strategic planning uncertainties, new competitors, and the potential for higher costs of doing business.

Uncertainty also brings financial hesitation: Typical investment activities, such as expanding operations, facility construction, and hiring and educating staff members tend to be some of the first areas that are shelved, until such time that stability resumes, representing a process that could take years. This uncertainty could put sales and profitability levels at risk, discarding any comfort that could be drawn from a company's historical financial performance; this can also impact business valuations significantly.

Yet, at the same time, periods of great change bring with them the opportunity to innovate and grow, but this requires new investment, an unwelcome reality for many business owners who are preferably looking towards succession and retirement. New business leaders must have the wherewithal to buy into a company, and at the same time, meet growth challenges or face the potential of implosion in the process. Challenges in this regard could include the need to do focused research, refine offerings, or implement services, while doing business with new customers in unfamiliar jurisdictions and uncharted territory. This type of growth also tends to require capital.

Closely related to these disruptions is the reality that business leaders and their successors can take only a limited amount of comfort in past financial results. Rapid change requires new business models and the marketplace has demonstrated that companies that do not keep pace with what their customers want could be quickly displaced by more savvy competitors. Think about the many well-known corporate names that have ceased business operations or significantly downsized in recent years.

New and Expensive Tax Risk. Add to all of this new and complex tax changes, such as restrictions in the areas of family income sprinkling and clawback of the small business deduction, which could impact profit margins and the ability of a company to save for its future. The uncertainty caused by these rules could also limit the level of reinvestment that pre-retirement stage owners are willing to make, or in the case of others, the ability to access capital, representing challenges to business innovation, growth, and value. These factors could directly impact succession planning and business transition activity, as uncertainty and diminished performance tend to lead to inaction.

Preparing for Explosive Change and Taking Control of the New Normal

Considering the alignment of these significant, macro-level trends in the new economy reinforces the fact that business leaders who are not ready to invest the necessary time and money have even less control over the future of their enterprise. It is nearly the perfect storm, as any one of these factors could severely impact a company's future, much less the pathway to survival when several are combined.

This also puts typical family business problems, such as conflict, relationships, ambiguity, and control issues into context. They remain, and simmer beneath the surface of the *The Family Business Time Bomb*, the latent risk within many companies, requiring only the tiniest of sparks to light the fuse.

Is the family business you work in under siege? In a distracted world of "selfies" and social media, how often do business leaders take the time to turn the camera away from the inner workings of their company, to instead focus on the shifting sands of what they have little ability to control: the world around them. This lack of balance between an internal and external focus makes it difficult to fully appreciate the dynamic environment that companies now face or the steps that should be taken in order to adapt to disruptive forces.

It is in this broader picture where *The Family Business Time Bomb* resides. A range of powerful components that have been quietly connecting themselves, and when combined, have the power to combust in a manner that many business leaders might not even recognize until it is too late. Leaving these challenges unaddressed increases the risk of ignition, resulting in what could be irreparable damage to the family business, its future, and the relationships that matter most.

But, there is some good news: if you are a family business leader, or hope to be one, it isn't too late to learn the necessary strategies to defuse the very volatile situation that your company – and your family—might be facing. This book will help you take control, combat the fuses that threaten your security, and in the process of doing so, manage risks to both your financial affairs and family relationships in these highly uncertain times, establishing a foundation for long term sustainability.

As you read this book, keep the following action-oriented steps in mind:

> **Step 1: Do your Homework:** Given the many shifts at both industry and market levels, it is critical to understand evolving trends,

opportunities, customer requirements, and consumption preferences, as it is this information that puts a company's capabilities in context. This process also involves being mindful of key challenges and risk areas, as well as developing strategies for how they could be overcome.

Step 2: Get your House in Order: Take a fresh look at your company, including products, services, systems, policies, procedures, cost structure, and resources. Is your business model positioned to benefit from marketplace opportunities, while addressing challenges and generating sufficient financial results? Utilize the findings of Step 1 to ensure that your company is structured in a manner that will lead to success and sustainability in the future. Fundamental to doing so is being in a position to identify and pursue the most appropriate marketplace opportunities with the right business model.

Step 3: Select New Opportunities, From a Position of Strength: Strategically building value puts companies in a better competitive position now, as well as when the time comes to sell, merge, or raise capital. These companies are also more likely to be relevant to the marketplace over the long term, and failing to do so puts a business at a significant risk of lacking the ability to be transitioned to someone else.

But, you cannot stop there, as implementation involves having the right strategy and action plan in place, as well as timely monitoring and correction. As simple as it might sound, failure often lies in poor execution; qualified advisors could be helpful, in terms of providing valuable solutions, perspective, and keeping the process on track.

The new way forward will not come from the founder alone, but rather, their actions today will determine whether or not the company has a future beyond the generation at hand. Decisions that business leaders make could have a profound impact on the ability of a company to provide for the family's income requirements over the long term; this is particularly true in the current new economy.

This reality means that there has never been a better time to take control of your company's future. Ready to get started? Then, let's go, or as we say: Ready? Set. Defuse!

JENIFER BARTMAN & EVELYN JACKS

1

A Bona Fide Market Driven Business
Why You Need to Get There, Now

Matthew and Blake, friends since elementary school, are both business owners in the construction industry. Blake, an electrician, has been working on job sites since the age of 18. He started his own business after spending a number of years working for others and is known for high quality work, reliability, and a friendly rapport with customers. Most of his jobs are found by word of mouth and he has a steady workload, which is especially busy during the summer months. Blake has not had to advertise; in fact, he sometimes has to turn away work, which he does not like to do, but there are not enough hours in the day to do otherwise. His wife handles the bookkeeping and coordinates his daily work schedule, allowing Blake to focus solely on the technical requirements and needs of his customers.

Matthew, a finishing carpenter, became interested in cabinetry while working in an upscale subdivision, eventually leaving his employment to purchase a small business from a founder who was near retirement and did not have a succession plan. His high quality, custom work is known for its unique designs, which allowed Matthew to build a product catalogue over the years, with each project he completed.

As his company grew, Matthew hired his two brothers; one as Sales Manager and the other as Production Manager, to support manufacture of a product line that is well suited to multi-unit dwellings, such as condominiums and the resurging rental market. After a few years of steady growth, Matthew and his brothers moved to a larger location and are currently considering future expansion. Since they have received inquiries from other parts of the country, they are also investigating distribution options to support sales in other geographic areas.

Blake is very happy for his friend, but often wonders why his company has not experienced a higher degree of growth and advancement.

THE ISSUES

Matthew and Blake are both family business owners, but there is a significant difference between the nature of their companies. Although both are successful, well regarded, and recognized for high quality work, their companies are operating on two different levels.

Blake learned a competency, such as a skill or trade, that could be readily sold in the marketplace, thereby creating a job for himself. His approach has essentially been to pursue at least the necessary amount of work to meet his family's economic requirements, often constrained by the capacity of "what can get done in a day". His company has been propelled by a single engine, occasionally assisted by part time support staff and employing a family member on a regular basis. In this scenario, a company can only drive so far, with limited carrying capability and speed.

Matthew, on the other hand, has taken a different approach to build his business, one that could be summarized as opportunity based. Although he might not even realize it, Matthew is driven by identifying and responding to needs in the marketplace, seeing things that "need doing" and determining how to capitalize. He is not averse to taking a risk to try something new and has the resourcefulness to fill knowledge gaps and transfer existing skills to new situations. His company has flourished as a result, in terms of sales, customers, and staff members, a situation that is analogous to a vehicle that fires on numerous engines, with capacity to propel and accelerate growth forward.

Positioning a company to capitalize on opportunity is one of the key characteristics of an entrepreneur. The Cambridge Dictionary defines an entrepreneur as "someone who starts their own business, especially when this involves seeing a new opportunity." The notion of "entrepreneur" and "entrepreneurial" tend to be overused, in a range of contexts, suggesting a green light for all things unstructured and flexible, where anything and everything goes, and all opportunities are worth pursuing.

In fact, the opposite is true. While "ideas" and "building" are of particular importance, a company will only flourish when a business leader's passions are focused and delivered within the context of a well-thought-out, tax-efficient business model and plan. Put another way, building an opportunity based company requires focus and discipline, and in the absence of this approach, many will (and do) fail.

To further our example, consider the following:

- Some companies exist to meet the economic needs of a person or family unit. The founder generates business within his or her network, which ultimately represents the company's customer base, and does not have significant initiative or capacity to grow beyond this point, as long as the family's economic needs are met. This type of company, illustrated by Blake's scenario, could be described as a **Lifestyle Business**.

- Some companies are opportunity driven, where the founder identifies unmet needs or areas of potential within the marketplace and seeks to position the business to benefit from these gaps. This approach could involve developing new products and services, delivering them in a manner that exceeds what is currently available, or perhaps, envisioning ways of doing things that do not currently exist. The founder is motivated to grow the company beyond the current economic needs of a person or family unit and might be driven by other factors, such as being an industry or market leader or recognized brand. This type of company, as illustrated by Matthew's scenario, could be described as a **Market Driven Business**.

Why is this an issue for you and your family business? Simply this: If your company is operating as a Lifestyle Business, rather than one that is market driven, all of the time, money, and energy that you invest in it might not be sufficient to achieve success over the long term. This limitation applies to a range of important areas, including market competitiveness, generating good financial results, and the potential for succession, in terms of transferring the company to someone else and generating a favourable return from doing so.

Many business owners take all of these areas for granted, and instead, focus their efforts on generating the next sale or addressing the customer that is in front of them. Little attention is paid to areas such as industry and market trends, changes in customer preferences, and the company's mid to long term strategy. What tends to happen is that a company begins to stray from the path of good business performance, with progress and results falling below that of full potential, becoming stagnant, or failing altogether. Whatever the trajectory, when a company is not operating at a strong performance level, it isn't the choice of customers, strategic partners, investors, or acquirors, representing a bad situation for everyone involved. This is particularly true in the current new economy of unprecedented change and disruption.

The good news is that business leaders can avoid this scenario, as long as they are committed to understanding the marketplace at hand, conducting an objective assessment of their company, identifying changes that should be made, and taking consistent action without delay. This process involves asking some tough questions about your ability to create, nurture, and grow your company, while addressing industry and market challenges, in a manner that will ensure long term success.

Starting at the heart of the matter: does the company have the ability in its current state to provide for, at a minimum, the economic needs of the family? Next, consider these relatively straightforward questions to obtain some quick, initial feedback on your company's level of horsepower:

- Is your company a leader in the marketplace?

- Does your company routinely take steps to investigate, develop, and pursue product and service offerings that represent the emerging position of your industry?

- Are the key functional areas in your company staffed by individuals (family members or otherwise) who are fully qualified to fulfil the role that they hold?

- Are your recruitment criteria based on hiring the best person for the role, regardless of whether or not they are a family member?

- Does your company have training and evaluation requirements to ensure that all staff members are qualified to do the job that they hold and are performing well, including family members?

- Does your company employ the right number of staff members to operate effectively, without any unnecessary or outdated positions?

- Does your company have a plan for investing in the necessary equipment, facilities, and technologies, to ensure that it is functioning well?

- Does your company have a current and fully developed business plan, including a financial forecast for a three to five-year period?

- Do you have the right planning and structures in place to minimize tax erosion?

- Does your company have a regularly functioning Board of Directors that includes individuals with a relevant skillset, at least some of whom are not family members?

- Do you have a group of qualified advisors, such as legal, accounting, tax, and business advisory, who work with the company on a regular basis?

If you answered "yes" to all or most of these questions, chances are that your company is well positioned to focus what is needed to be successful in its marketplace—a Market Driven Business.

If you answered "no" to all or most of these questions, chances are that your company is best characterized as a Lifestyle Business, where the main focus thus far has been on providing for the economic needs of an individual or family unit.

The Bottom Line: If your company is a Lifestyle Business, your investment in it might be at risk. Why? Because without a definitive plan to understand emerging trends and developments, grow revenues, efficiently manage expenses, and maximize your company's equity and cash flow, the risk of erosion by competitive forces, taxes, and marketplace challenges might be too significant to overcome.

Put another way, in an increasingly competitive environment, it is critical to ensure that an appropriate business model and plan are in place (and being executed well) in order to raise the likelihood of the company being a good candidate for transition to someone else in the future. Since there are a limited number of potential successors and acquirors, *they* have the opportunity to choose from a range of companies, with many being left behind in the process. Building a company that is relevant to the marketplace has never been more important, if long term, sustainable wealth creation is the goal.

However, if your company is currently operating as a Lifestyle Business, with a desire to move to a market driven level, it won't happen without a firm commitment to do the work.

THE SOLUTIONS

Making the shift from a Lifestyle Business to a Market Driven Business is not an easy one, nor will it happen overnight. It requires a thorough understanding of the key attributes of companies that are marketplace leaders—those that consistently provide and/or develop product and service offerings that are driven by the needs and wants of customers, as opposed to focusing on what is most convenient for the family. And this transition will not happen without a plan.

As a starting point, all companies require a baseline of fundamental business practices, regardless of their age or size. This includes:

- A current and well developed **business plan** that outlines the goals, objectives, core activities and strategies, as well as projected financial results for a three to five year period. A business plan **must** be built upon an appropriate business model and a strategy that is outlined in the context of the industry, market, and target market(s) that are relevant to the company; failing to do so is a common weakness.

- An **annual operating plan and budget** that includes the goals and core activities for the year, as well as projected financial results on at least a monthly and annual basis.

- The necessary **systems, policies, procedures, and resources** to support efficient and effective operations, at a day-to-day, strategic, and governance level

These critical items, the details of which will not be considered here, are the starting point for establishing the foundation upon which a company should be built. Some business leaders might gloss over these areas, perhaps with the viewpoint of being "nice to have" or "good ideas that don't apply to my company"; this couldn't be further from the truth. Failing to invest the time and energy to establish and maintain these fundamental business practices is analogous to building on unstable ground, providing insufficient support for growth-oriented initiatives.

Many business leaders have learned this lesson the hard way, such as when attempting to raise capital or attract strategic partners without success. They wonder why no one is interested in their offering, failing to realize just how uncompetitive it is, as compared to the companies that have followed good advice and taken the necessary steps to get to a position of strength. Failing to do so also puts a company in a poor position to withstand the new economy challenges of rapid change and uncertainty.

Once a company has its foundation in place, it is in a position to develop what could be described as a Business Transformation Plan, to move the company to a market driven level.

The Business Transformation Plan

A Business Transformation Plan provides the roadmap for moving a Lifestyle Business to a market driven state. Using a company's well developed business plan as a starting point, it addresses many of the topics that are discussed in this book, including:

- The level of family involvement, in terms of roles, responsibilities, and ownership
- Performance management requirements and expectations
- Strategy for engaging non-family members
- Planning for succession, in terms of roles, responsibilities, and transfer of the entity
- Growth-oriented options, such as raising capital, strategic partnerships, and transactions

In order to develop an effective approach for maximizing family wealth, these key strategy and decision points should be supported by technical considerations, in terms of the tax implications of managing a company on an ongoing basis, saving, investing, and as a result of business transactions.

The suggested approach for building a Business Transformation Plan is to conduct a "gap" analysis in each of the key areas, whereby a company's current state is documented and compared to the desired state, as outlined in this book. The difference between these two states (the gap) is identified and action-oriented recommendations are then developed. This approach is helpful, as it allows business leaders to see and understand not only where modifications are required, but also in terms of a clear and action-oriented plan that indicates what the next steps should be. Depending on the extent and nature of the action plan steps, a timeline for completion could also be developed.

The Business Transformation Planning Process

As a family business leader, you are not only the expert of your company, but also in terms of your family unit. This situation could result in challenging and sometimes conflicting perspectives, particularly since close family relationships are a significant part of the mix. You might recognize, after careful consideration, that a Lifestyle Business is no longer sufficient to meet the economic needs of the family, resulting in the need to shift to a market driven approach. This type of transition could involve some difficult decisions that must be made in the best interest of the company, and ultimately, the family and its financial future.

Facing this type of situation alone could be particularly stressful, as the impact of personal relationships on decision making might result in changes that should be made not occurring, limiting the company's ability to evolve to the necessary competitive position to generate success in the marketplace. This puts the family's economic well-being at risk, as changes that would yield financially beneficial results have been undermined, in an attempt to preserve short term harmony.

A common example of this scenario is a parent who is trying to plan for how the company that they founded should be transferred to their children. Since dividing a company into multiple parts is not always feasible or desirable, the absence of a decision, while adult children wear a path in the floor to Dad's office, each making the case as to why they should benefit the most, too often yields no progress, the result of which tends to be unfavourable for the business. Why does this happen? Although there can be a range of reasons, an important one relates to feelings of isolation and a lack of trust, in making such an important and complex decision. Business leaders also tend to not make changes unless they can identify a solution that addresses concerns around "fairness".

A better way to move towards a market driven approach is to engage an independent business advisor to guide the process and provide decision making support. You might currently have someone in your advisory network that has the ability to fulfill this role, or you might wish to engage someone who is new to the situation. One of the benefits of a new business advisor is that they typically bring a fresh perspective and are often in a better position to identify issues or opportunities that might not have already been recognized. They could also bring the benefit of being truly independent, without preconceived ideas or history with the company, family members, or existing advisors, representing a level of objectivity with new clarity and credibility.

Regardless, whomever you select as a business advisor to lead the process should have the necessary qualifications and an established track record in terms of business planning, financial management, and operational experience (i.e., managing a company). Knowledge and experience in the areas of project and transition management, human resources, tax matters, and business financing (raising capital, transactions, succession planning, etc.) are helpful, as shifting to a Market Driven Business will include most, if not all, of these issues. In addition, it is critical that the business advisor understands the company from a holistic perspective (as opposed to being limited to a functional area), as well as in terms of identifying and capitalizing on market trends and opportunities.

Once an advisor has been identified, meet with them to discuss expectations, in terms of timelines, objectives, and how they could best assist you during the process. Once this has been established, review and discuss your current business plan and identify the need for any updates, as well as the process for documenting your company's current state within each of the gap analysis areas. Depending on the company's particular circumstances, additional categories to review and consider tend to become apparent.

It is also important to identify any areas where there is a lack of information, in terms of moving forward. Despite having conducted a thorough business planning process, it still might be desirable to have a better understanding of the trends and areas of opportunity within your industry, to identify those that the company should pursue. Your business advisor should be able to assist you with identifying and accessing relevant information and sources, as well as the basis for evaluation and selection. Whatever the issue, business leaders should not be hesitant to identify "blind spots", as doing so is a prerequisite for successful growth. Understanding this is extremely important, as those who fail to do so are limited by their own knowledge and experience, not recognizing that greater capacity is needed to build and maintain a market driven company.

You are now ready to embark upon the process of developing a Business Transformation Plan, to assess the position of your company, as compared to the profile of a Market Driven Business, from which an action plan for moving forward could be developed.

Read on, as we discuss the key areas to understand, consider, and address.

SUMMARY: DEFUSING THE FAMILY BUSINESS TIME BOMB
Minefields

- Focusing solely on family member personalities and circumstances has a good chance of leading to the wrong decision, or perhaps no decision at all. One of the complications with family businesses is that they involve close personal relationships, which tend to impact decision making, and often, not for the better (especially in terms of the company's best interests).

- If the intent is to move from a Lifestyle Business to a Market Driven Business, do not go it alone. Chances are, you will be faced with some challenging decision points and might find yourself at odds with family members, at least for the short term. An experienced business advisor could keep the transformation process on track, manage personalities, and act as an objective support and sounding board.

Tools

- View the company as a means to provide for the family's economic needs. Instead of focusing on family member personalities and relationships, think about the company as an engine: evaluate its efficiency, how well it operates, and the type of performance that it generates (i.e., financial, tax, and other results). Ask yourself if the existing engine is functioning in the manner that it should or if an overhaul is needed. Is the company a one engine vehicle or does it have a more robust level of fuel power to take flight and move it forward?

- Think about what would happen if the company no longer existed; how would the family's economic needs be met? Consider this in terms of choosing between "the lesser of two evils", in a sense that making significant changes might result in long-term survival and growth, as opposed to current performance levels or a future characterized by stagnation and decline.

- Be realistic about the impact of the new economy, as change and new ways of doing business are here to stay. Keeping the external environment top of mind will put the company and family expectations in context and grounded in reality.

- Give yourself some time to consider the situation, recognizing that significant change does not have to occur immediately or all at once. Having said that, give yourself a reasonable time limit to determine your course of action and move to the next step.

YOUR MISSION: A Bona Fide Market Driven Business. Why you need to get there, now.

READY THINGS YOU NEED TO KNOW

- Both Lifestyle and Market Driven businesses could be successful and well regarded. The key issue is determining: (i) the approach that is required to meet, and perhaps exceed, the family's economic needs, both now and in the future; and (ii) if there are "greater things" that you wish to achieve.

- Failure to determine if your company is in a position to meet the family's future financial requirements and implementing the necessary business and tax strategies puts their well-being at risk.

- In order for your company to compete at a market driven level, focus on what is necessary to do so, as opposed to on what is most convenient for the family. When making business related decisions, what is in the best interest of the company should ultimately prevail.

SET QUESTIONS YOU NEED TO ASK

- Is my company a Lifestyle Business or a Market Driven Business?

- Am I satisfied with the category in which the company currently falls?

- Is the company currently meeting the financial needs of the family?

- What is the company's performance outlook for the next several years?

- If the objective is to move to the market driven category, what could some of the impacts be on the family, both positive and negative?

- If the company continues to operate as a Lifestyle Business, what would it look like in 5 years', 10 years', and 20 years' time? Would it be able to provide for the family's economic needs? Would the company continue to exist?

- How would the family's economic needs be met if the company could no longer function?

THINGS YOU NEED TO DO

- Determine if you alone have the skills, time, and energy to re-position the company.

- Determine if you currently have a qualified business advisor who could assist you in developing a Business Transformation Plan.

- Review the company's financial performance for the last five years, paying careful attention to trends in terms of, revenue, expenses, profitability, and cash flow. Identify whether the company is in a state of growth, stability, or decline.

- Develop a highlevel forecast of the company's financial performance for the next three to five years. Identify whether it is expected to be in a state of growth, stability, or decline.

- Determine if additional capital is likely to be required, and if so, how it could be provided.

DEFUSE DECISIONS YOU NEED TO MAKE

- Determine if you need or have a desire to take the necessary steps to move your company from a Lifestyle Business to a Market Driven Business.

- Select a business advisor(s) to assist you with the process.

✔ **Mission Accomplished:** When a family business leader is able to make the distinction between positioning the company to capitalize on market opportunities for the benefit of the family, as opposed to structuring and managing it solely based on what is most convenient for family members, the basis exists for generating real wealth over the long term. Someone should reap the benefits of marketplace opportunities—why not your business?

2

Building Business Value
When Equity Extraction is the Goal

Arianne is a successful investment advisor who grew up in a family business environment. Her parents, George and Mia, started a restaurant when she was a young child that eventually grew to include a food production facility that prepares and distributes some of their most successful recipes. She worked in the company as a teenager, while attending university, eventually leaving for full time employment with an investment firm in another part of the country. Her brother, Nick, continued to work in the business, assisting his parents in various capacities as the company grew.

By her own admission, Arianne wishes she could spend more time with her family. Her periodic visits home are always busy and tend to pass quickly, with lots of enthusiastic discussion about how well the company is doing, including achievement of various awards and community recognition. Arianne noticed on her last visit that her parents both seemed tired, as they chatted about their retired friends and the vacations they were able to take, including back to their childhood homes to visit family and enjoy the sites. She wasn't entirely surprised to receive a phone call from her father soon after she returned to her condo in the city, asking when she could make an impromptu trip home to discuss selling the business.

Arianne arranged to spend a week with her family about a month later, to review the status of the company and offer some advice. Upon arriving, she was taken aback by a number of things, including the condition of the plant; it had barely changed from when she left 15 years ago, now seeming archaic and in need of a significant upgrade. The finances were also concerning, and although revenue levels were reasonably steady, the company's margins and cash position were well below what she would have expected. Staring out the window, Arianne thought about what she had observed of her family's lifestyle: luxury vehicles, a summer cottage, Nick's new motorcycle; and what on earth she was going to say to her parents.

THE ISSUES

The family business scenario described above is one that is quite common. A founder (or founders) start a company at a relatively young age, fulfilling a fairly basic market need that arises from their knowledge, capability, or even a personal interest or hobby. They get family members working alongside, invest lots of time and effort, and take opportunities as they come. Fast forward several years and they have what appears to be a thriving business, supporting the family's needs as they grow with the company over time. In some instances, the family is savvy enough to pursue new and different opportunities, such as in this case, expanding into food production and distribution.

The outcome that is described here is also quite common. A company grows and the family enjoys the trappings that often come with success: a larger home, more expensive vehicles, travel, a vacation property, and perhaps, enhanced education for their children. At this stage, the years could pass quite quickly, with thoughts of retirement or "what's next?" eventually becoming part of the conversation.

Once business leaders start to think about this next stage, one of the most common questions is "how much could I get for my company?" This consideration is sometimes fueled by a business owner friend who "hit the jackpot" by selling their company, which tends to set the standard for others. These situations are often not the norm, but rather, represent an exceptionally well managed and positioned enterprise, or perhaps, a buyer who considers the company to be of strategic importance (more about that later). The reality is that many, if not most, family businesses are not currently in a position to generate the level of value upon sale that founders expect. Why is this the case?

Using our example to provide an explanation, the simple answer is this: business leaders tend to build their companies in a manner that lacks what is required in order to generate a high level of value upon transaction. They also tend to do things that result in a *decline* in value, such as not investing in facilities and capital assets (resulting in an outdated and inefficient plant), failing to manage costs efficiently, not updating their business model, and having insufficient cash to support growth.

These areas are actually symptoms of deeper issues, including shortfalls in the areas of systems, policies, procedures, and people, which could range from less than ideal to severely inadequate. Companies could also fall behind the trends and developments that impact their industry and marketplace, leaving them with products that are not at the top of a customer's list. Trends could also significantly impact a company's business model, in terms of the manner in which money is made from products and services, falling out of step with changes in consumer behavior and consumption patterns.

Founders could easily get in the habit of extracting cash from the company to support their own personal lifestyle, as opposed to reinvesting back into the business to build value. As the years pass, these cash withdrawals are essentially a transfer of wealth to the business owner on a personal level, an accumulation of various assets and cash to fund lifestyle related expenditures. Where does this leave the company when it is time to sell?

The Bottom Line: Founders could spend years, if not a good portion of their lives, working on building their business. As owners, the value of doing so is not typically realized until their shares in the company are sold or transferred to someone else. Business owners are often dismayed when they receive purchase offers that seem well below what they believe the company's value to be, resulting in a difficult and sobering crossroads.

Value could either be built inside a company or extracted from it. How, when, and if this happens depends on the actions that business leaders take over the course of their ownership tenure.

THE SOLUTIONS

In order to realize on all of the hard work and effort that a founder puts into building a business, it is important to do so in a manner that builds value *within the company*, not somewhere else. Let's consider what this means in practical terms.

- Companies that are **dependent on the knowledge, skill, and network of the founder** are generally of limited value when it comes to transition. Why? Because when the founder leaves the company, they essentially take the business' ability to function with them, leaving the entity worth little on its own.

- When a founder **transfers a significant portion of the cash that is generated by a business to themselves** on a regular basis (perhaps, by way of a dividend to a holding company), there is little remaining capital to invest into its operations and generate growth. In this type of situation, the company tends to be worth little in relation to selling, as the business owner has essentially extracted the bulk of its value over time.

- Business leaders who have **an abundance of ideas or "potential", in terms of what could be done to enhance their products and services, but do not take action to do so,** have not added value to their company. Put another way, the homeowner who dreams about building an addition to their house, but never does will not get value for it when selling the property, as buyers do not pay others for things that they would ultimately have to do themselves.

- Companies that **lack infrastructure, such as updated and well-functioning capital assets and facilities,** as well as staff and management team members who are well trained and possess the necessary knowledge and skills to perform admirably are of little value. If an acquiror must invest their own capital and effort in order to bring these areas up to the appropriate performance level, they will not pay upon purchase, to reward a founder for what is essentially neglect and a lack of attention to these important areas.

- Business leaders who **do not devote sufficient time to stay up to date with industry and marketplace developments** run the risk of ending up with products and services that are not of relevance to customers. This type of situation often results in a decreased level of sales over time, contributing to a decline in value. Companies in this situation might not have a future, resulting in wind up and closure being the only option.

- Needs in the marketplace are driven by what customers want and the manner in which they procure and consume products and services. If a company **does not take proactive action to understand and adapt to changes in consumer behavior,** it could quickly find its business model out of date, being displaced by talented competitors. A basic example of this scenario is a company that lacks a well-developed online and social media presence, to support and generate sales in the new economy.

All of these examples represent situations where a founder or business leader has not seized the opportunity to build value, accelerate growth, and ultimately be compensated for doing so upon sale of the company. Although business leaders might understand the shortfalls in these areas, *it does not mean that they have the ability to create a different outcome;* this is where advisors could be helpful.

Business leaders need to plan ahead and fully understand the approaches for creating and realizing value and the strategies that need to be in place in order to get there. This is the only way to create a business that is a viable, going concern, representing a good candidate for transfer to someone else, as opposed to a company that doesn't have a future beyond its current state. Too many founders find themselves in this situation, often unexpectedly and too late.

Considering what needs to be done in order to make a company a candidate for successful transition involves not only addressing the above noted areas, but also mastering the topics that are covered in this book, including managing family member involvement, engaging non-family members, generating strong performance, and protecting against the impact of crisis and risk situations. It is also important to keep up with industry and market developments, as well as the challenges and opportunities of economic, financial, and political factors, especially in the current times of uncertainty and evolution.

All of these areas are beyond the typical day-to-day focus, which tends to receive the majority of a family business leader's time and effort. This is why it is so important for business leaders to get in the habit of allocating a portion of their time to focus on strategic matters, with the objective of building value in their company on a sustainable basis. This includes identifying gaps and necessary action items to bring the company to a market driven level of development.

Building Business Value

When considering the topic of building value, it is important for founders and business leaders to recognize that potential successors and acquirors *have a choice* in terms of selecting a company in which to invest. From the perspective of a purchaser or investor, there are at least two points of view when considering opportunities:

- **Pay a "good to great" level of value** for a company that is well established and in a strong position to generate favourable financial results for the foreseeable future (in other words, buy a house that is in good condition and doesn't require a significant amount of renovation and upgrade in the short term); or

- **Pay a relatively low level of value** for a company with potential, but where investment is needed in order to bring it up to an appropriate level (analogous to buying a property in a good location, where significant upgrades are needed in order to get the house to where its condition and corresponding value should be).

Business leaders who seek to receive a "good to great" level value of value upon transition need to ensure that their company is sufficiently developed in order to be worthy of it. Business leaders that have not sufficiently invested in the company, to ensure that it is functioning well and is in a position to grow and generate good financial results going forward, tend to find themselves in the second category, where an acquiror would only be willing to pay a relatively low value. Keep in mind that many of the companies in this category might not be saleable at all, leaving the only options as being retained by the business leader or wound up and closed.

Let's consider some of the fundamental things that must be put in place to support establishing meaningful value within a company *prior* to transition. Areas to address include the following:

- **Industry and market trends**—In order for a company to be relevant in the marketplace, it must have products and services that effectively meet needs, delivered in a manner that customers want. This involves understanding developments in the industry and market, including areas such as product development, technological advancement, changes in consumer preferences and consumption, as well as competitive offerings. Fully understanding these areas on an ongoing basis allows a business leader to ensure that their company is positioned to be a leader, with relevant products, services, and distribution methods that are the choice of customers.

- **Business Model**—A company's business model is the manner in which it "makes money" by responding to needs in the marketplace. For most companies, there are various approaches that could be taken in developing a business model (i.e., sales could be generated online, by way of the company's own salesforce, through distribution partners, retail, wholesale, etc.); the challenge is to select the approach(es) that best meet customer needs and combat competitive forces. Business models could be appropriate for a period of time, but require revision (or a complete overhaul) due to industry or market changes. Failing to do so could leave a once thriving business behind the rest of the marketplace, such as in situations where technology has a particularly pronounced impact.

- **Systems**—Companies that lack core systems tend to operate inefficiently, such as in the areas of manufacturing, production, information, sales, financial, and resources management. A common example is when a company undergoes a significant level of growth, but is still "managed" with systems that are typical of a much smaller organization. Business leaders could find themselves frustrated with a lack of reliable and timely information, leading to poor decision making and uncertainty around the steps that should be taken to improve the situation. Companies that generate good value upon transition have core systems that are current, well populated, and able to generate reliable information on a timely basis. This represents a meaningful investment in the company and acquirors will not pay a good level of value in situations where this work becomes part of their own "to do" list.

- **Policies and Procedures**—This area is analogous to a restaurant having a robust recipe catalogue covering a full menu range, with a list of ingredients, preparation, and cooking instructions for each item. This valuable catalogue ensures that the restaurant is in a position to deliver a great dining experience to patrons that doesn't require "starting from scratch" every time, providing all of the necessary guidelines to whoever might be working in the kitchen on a given day.

Conversely, imagine what it would be like to dine at a restaurant where all of this knowledge resided within the mind of an individual or two, and the meal that might be delivered if they were not working that day. Sound ridiculous? The reality is that many small companies are managed in this manner, without documented policies and procedures and largely reliant upon the business leader. It should not be surprising that companies of this nature do not yield much in the way of value upon sale, especially when compared to other options.

- **People**—Family businesses are particularly prone to "people issues", which are discussed further in future chapters. Notwithstanding the obvious fact that jobs are not performed well if they are held by people who lack the right qualifications, knowledge, and ability, this area must also be addressed in conjunction with changing times, in terms of a company's industry, market, and business model.

It is very common for founders to become complacent with the staff members around them, failing to recognize situations where a role has become increasingly large or complex (a typical example is finance). What results is a situation where a role "passes by" the capability of the current staff member, resulting in poor performance at both a personal and organizational level. Companies that lack a staff and management team that is complete, well qualified, and performing well in their roles are unlikely to generate a good level of value upon sale, as the acquiror would be required to resolve these weaknesses post-transaction. This area is one that tends to be extremely time consuming, which is why talented staff members should be viewed as an investment.

- **Financial Performance**—In order for a company to generate good financial results, it typically must be operating well in most, if not all, of the areas mentioned above. Like a championship sports team, success is unlikely if strength does not exist at all positions, as well as in terms of coaching and training resources. Business leaders will sometimes decide that it is "time to sell" after they have had a particularly good year, only to be surprised to learn that they are unable to attract a buyer who will pay the desired purchase price. Why is this the case?

Experienced acquirors recognize that a year or two of strong performance does not make a great company, nor does it justify a high value upon sale. Companies are "going concerns" and are sold on the basis that they will continue to operate, and a significant portion of establishing their value is often based on future financial results. Accordingly, companies must establish a *track record* of favourable performance for a much longer period of time, five to seven years, at a minimum, in order to justify sustainability and a higher level of value upon sale.

- **Tax Efficiency**—In order to maximize performance over time, companies should have appropriate tax planning strategies in place, so that as much of each dollar that is earned as possible is also retained. As with any other strategic area, business leaders are often so consumed by operational matters that they lack the time to focus on longer term areas, resulting in a financial track record that is less than ideal. In addition to ongoing tax advice, it is also beneficial to understand the options for structuring a business leader's exit from a company, to maximize gains in a tax efficient manner.

As part of the transformation planning process, business leaders should work with their advisor to assess all of these important areas, in terms of the following:

- Documenting the company's **current state**;

- Comparing the current state to what represents **appropriate business practices**; and

- Developing an **action plan to close the gap** between the two states

Recognize that this could represent an ongoing process, as the industry, market, competitive landscape, and other external factors continue to change and evolve. The action plan that is developed tends to include many tasks and should utilize a process that is "evergreen", to complete items and identify new areas to address.

This approach puts a company in a much better position to perform well and be of relevance for the future, if not, regarded as a marketplace leader, if they make the effort to undertake the necessary work to reach this level. It is these companies that are typically of interest to external parties, such as potential successors, acquirors, strategic partners, and investors, as they are in the best position to generate strong financial results going forward, representing an opportunity to generate a favourable return on investment (ROI).

To put this in a slightly different context, seasoned acquirors and investors understand the difference between what could be referred to as financial value and strategic value, which could be defined as follows:

- **Financial Value** is based on what an item costs.

- **Strategic Value** is based on what an item costs, plus something extra. In the case of a business, strategic value might include areas such as a recognized brand name, a gap that it could fill in the acquiror's existing product line, a strong product development function, or the ability to combine resources in a manner that decreases costs or creates efficiencies.

Companies that not only build value, but also do so in a manner that represents strategic value have a better opportunity to maximize their sale price. This is because they are in a position to deliver additional benefits, including a higher likelihood of building value in the future.

Arriving at a position of strategic value is a tall order, but this achievement is well worth the effort. At the same time, it is critical to recognize that value is not a given and could vary over time, with changes in the industry, market, competitive landscape, and the company's performance. As a result, just because a company is estimated to be worth a particular amount at a point in time **does not mean** that this level of value would hold into the future. It is important to keep building a company in a manner that positions it to continue to generate value, as when it comes to selling a business, the money is not in the bank until the owner "cashes out".

Family Considerations

One thing that readers might be wondering at this point is something along the lines of "since this is a family business book, what are the value implications when the successor is a family member?" In some instances, founders might take the view that they wish to transition their company to a family member for a "fair" price, one that is not as high as if the business was sold to an external party. If this is the case, there are two things that a founder should keep in mind: (i) they have the latitude to accept a price that is less than what could be generated in an external transaction, however; (ii) the company still must be functioning well enough to justify what the founder considers to be "fair value" (in other words, a family member successor is not going to pay in abundance to take on the founder's headache of a company).

In the event that a founder's objective is to maximize value, regardless of who the purchaser is, this is not likely to happen without paying sufficient attention to the areas discussed in this chapter. Founders put their heart and soul into building their businesses and it is a reasonable expectation that they should benefit from doing so. Passing a strong company to the next generation also puts them in a better position to be successful going forward, however, a successor's opportunity to generate wealth is on the road ahead, which might not be consistent with what has occurred during the founder's time at the helm.

Family member successors sometimes do not fully appreciate this point, especially if they are employed in the company prior to transition. They question the rationale of working hard to help make the company successful, which could result in a higher value being paid during the transfer of ownership at a future point in time. This perspective begs the question: "what would you rather have: a company that is well situated for success or one that is in a poor position to generate wealth going forward?" The answer should be an easy one, but unfortunately, this basic logic sometimes gets lost in the process of considering transition of a family business.

SUMMARY: DEFUSING THE FAMILY BUSINESS TIME BOMB

Minefields

- Being dismissive about the importance of fundamental business practices, such as systems, policies, and procedures is a sure-fire way to not build value in a company. Business leaders who take the viewpoint that these practices are "for bigger companies" or are "good ideas, but not something that we have to do" are only fooling themselves. Potential successors and acquirors will view this lack of attention as a weakness, resulting in tasks that they would have to address themselves post-transaction.

- Business leaders need to be definitive about when they intend to depart their role or sell the company. Those who kick the can down the road with vague commentary such as "maybe in five years" do a disservice to building value in the company, lacking a tangible goal to work towards, among other things.

- Founders tend to overestimate the value that their company would generate upon sale. A better approach is to get a reliable estimate from a qualified valuation professional well in advance of the exit timeframe and work towards building and maintaining value.

Tools

- It could be challenging to obtain a good understanding of where your company is currently at, in terms of areas that build value. A qualified business advisor could provide an objective viewpoint, as well as battle-tested strategies for improvement.

- It is much easier to make transformation planning progress by keeping the action plan and implementation process moving forward, as stopping and starting tends to be inefficient, expensive, and frustrating. If you lack the time to lead the process, delegate this role to someone with sufficient project management and implementation experience (your business advisor could also be helpful in this regard).

- It is important to recognize that building value is an ongoing part of a company's strategy, as marketplace changes could impact what was once considered to be of value.

YOUR MISSION:
Building Business Value. When equity extraction is the goal.

READY THINGS YOU NEED TO KNOW

- Business leaders should have a strategy to build value in their company over the course of their tenure, in order to generate favourable financial results and a successful transition.

- Potential successors, acquirors, and investors typically have a range of opportunities from which they could select. Although their personal objectives and mandates might vary, companies that are of limited value are not likely to be candidates of interest, nor will they yield a good sale price.

- Value is not a given and could vary over time, with changes in the industry, market, competitive landscape, and a company's performance.

SET QUESTIONS YOU NEED TO ASK

- Do I have a realistic understanding of the current value of my company?

- Am I satisfied with the current value of my company?

- Does the company operate in a manner that demonstrates a good understanding of current industry, market, and competitive trends?

- Is the company's business model in step with the industry and market and sufficient to generate good financial results?

- Are the company's systems up to date and functioning well?

- Does the company have appropriate policies and procedures in all important areas?

- Have policies and procedures been implemented and enforced?

- Does the company have people with the right qualifications, skills, and experience in all roles?

- Is the company generating good financial results?

- For what length of time does the company have a track record of strong financial performance?

- Does the company have a tax planning strategy in place, for both ongoing operations and upon transition?

- What level of value would the company likely generate upon transition? Financial value? Strategic value?

THINGS YOU NEED TO DO

- Review the areas in this chapter, in terms of business transformation planning.

- Develop an action plan of tasks that need to be addressed, including timing and responsibility for each item.

- Identify areas where you lack the time and/or experience to address and discuss options for resolution with your business advisor.

- Review your company's existing tax planning process and resources.

- Meet with your tax advisor (or engage one, as required) to enhance the company's tax planning strategy.

- If you do not have a realistic understanding of your company's estimated value, seek out qualified valuation resources that could assist in this area.

`DEFUSE` DECISIONS YOU NEED TO MAKE

- Determine the level of importance of generating a good to great level of value upon the sale of your ownership position or company. If this is important to you, it is not likely to occur without a concerted effort to build value within the business. Determine whether or not you are willing to take the necessary steps to do so, based on the outcome of the business transformation planning process.

- Identify and commit to a realistic timeframe in terms of when you intend to exit from the company or sell the business.

✔ **Mission Accomplished:** If you build it well, they will come (acquirors, that is). When looking to buy or assume the leadership role of a company, successors and acquirors tend to have more options than available capital or resources. As a result, the best, most desirable opportunities tend to receive the greatest level of attention, and ultimately, are chosen. When a business leader understands that their task is to build a company that not only operates well, but is also positioned to be the choice of acquirors and successors, not to mention customers, they are in a position to generate long term wealth, including upon transition.

3

The Tricky Minefield of Family Involvement
Managing Starry Eyed Aspirations

Vicky started a floral design business 10 years ago with the goal of supporting herself and her two young children. Recently divorced, Vicky needed to create an income for herself, a challenge, since she had been a stay-at-home mother for a number of years. Her children, Ashley and Aidan, now aged 20 and 18, watched her build the business from a part-time initiative, developed from Vicky's enthusiasm for floral design courses taken in the evenings at a local art college, to a bustling enterprise employing 25 staff members in a retail shop and an online order and delivery service.

Vicky spent a considerable amount of time over the years building the company, with her days consumed by customer and supplier meetings and evenings with administrative and bookkeeping tasks. It was not unusual for her to set aside her laptop to help her children with their homework, or for business calls to interrupt the dinner hour. Vicky was the heart of the business, its driving force, and not a single floral arrangement went out the door without her approval.

As the company continued to grow, bringing challenges with every new customer, it became evident that Vicky needed some help. She had plenty of front line staff members, but was often overwhelmed by the growing administrative, management, and supervisory responsibilities. She thought that getting her children involved in the business was an obvious solution, providing the opportunity to bring in staff members with the same attention to detail and passion for the company, as well as trustworthy resources that would instinctively know how to do things right.

Vicky considered Aidan, in his first year of management studies at university, less likely to become involved. Ashley, currently studying interior design, would be well suited to join the company, although she had never expressed an interest in doing so. Ashley did, however, often comment on the many events that Vicky attended, to either set up floral arrangements or as a thank you from happy customers; this struck her as being "quite the life". Despite an impressive closet full of pretty dresses and shoes and fun filled social media accounts, Vicky knew that this was not always as glamourous as it could be perceived, as it led to long days and work for which she wasn't always compensated.

"No matter", Vicky thought to herself, "Ashley is a natural fit and will figure it out. She's so much like me!".

THE ISSUES

Vicky's story is not an unusual one; a business that is born out of economic necessity experiences growth beyond the founder's expectations and capacity. Years go by, characterized by the company's daily requirements and family obligations consuming every waking moment, and although most business owners do their best to maintain some level of control and balance, they still might find themselves living in a 24-hour blur most of the time. Some founders describe this feeling as one where things could careen out of control at any moment, but are often too busy to do anything meaningful about it. Hanging on for dear life is like that.

Even though they were not actively involved in the company, it was a significant presence in the lives of Vicky's children, who saw their mother strive to complete all of the tasks that she needed to accomplish in a day, from the time they were very young. Their lives were interrupted when the business needed attention, and whether Vicky realizes it or not, it's likely that her children have already formulated their own opinions of the company, including their level of interest and what a closer relationship with it could mean to their future. Chances are, she does not have a good grasp on this issue, and perhaps, like many business owners, has been too busy building the company to give it much consideration.

Like many founders, Vicky is facing a significant problem, despite many years of hard work and effort: she has not taken steps to build depth in the company, which is fundamental to transitioning a Lifestyle Business to a market driven level. In the process, she has overextended herself, to a point where she is the company, similar to a child that cannot survive without a parent. Put another way, companies in this situation are dependent on the business leader.

The growth of the company is constrained by what Vicky alone can accomplish in a management capacity, setting the stage for missed sales opportunities, substandard customer service, and decreased product quality, all of which represent risks to the business' financial success, sustainability, and ultimate value. Further, she has not taken any tangible steps to mentor her perceived successor, and there is no evidence of her children having an interest in this role, beyond Vicky's own expectations. In fact, it might actually be too late to build this link.

Vicky has two key challenges to consider:

First, family member involvement and/or business succession is likely not an option in Vicky's situation. Since she has not engaged her children in an ongoing discussion about their potential involvement in the company, Ashley and Aidan have not had an opportunity to learn firsthand about the business and the opportunities it presents. They might even have assumed that she has other plans and directed their interests elsewhere as a result.

Second, Vicky does not have a formal, realistic growth or succession plan, as she has been focused solely on operating the business and practicing little more than "imaginary succession" when it comes to her children and the role they might play. This situation represents a significant risk to the future of the company, as she has not taken steps to explore and develop alternate succession options or fully understand the level of interest from family members.

In order to address this situation, Vicky should take steps to answer the following questions, preferably with the help of professional advisors:

- What is the company's growth plan for the foreseeable future (i.e., for the next one, three, and five years, as well as on a long term basis)?

- Are there particular trends and developments in the industry, market, or external environment that could represent a significant opportunity or threat for the company in the future?

- Is the involvement of one or both of her children the best option for generating future growth in the company?

- Are they well-suited to and interested in becoming involved in the company?

- What role(s) in the company could they fulfill, with the necessary education and experience?

- Would they have an interest in obtaining the necessary qualifications and experience?

- How would involvement of one child, but not the other, impact the siblings and their relationship?

- How would this impact dynamics within the family unit as a whole?

- What other steps should be taken to position the company to operate on a market driven level?

- What are Vicky's plans for her own future, in terms of remaining in the company?

- What other options does she have, in terms of succession and transition of the company, in the event that involving her children is not feasible?

The Bottom Line: Vicky needs answers, that speak to the present, future, and are rooted firmly in reality. Just because a founder spends years passionately building their company, in the presence of family members and other relatives, does not mean that they share her feelings or interests, or that they have a realistic understanding of what is involved. In the absence of having meaningful conversations, in terms of expectations, potential for involvement, and future ownership, founders are left only with their dreams, which might not reflect reality.

THE SOLUTIONS

What could Vicky have done differently to avoid this very common situation?

The starting point is to build a company that is not dependent on its leader and is positioned to operate on a market driven level. In the case of companies that operate as a Lifestyle Business in their early years, founders need to recognize the limitations of this approach and what is required in order to undertake the transformation process. Critical to this is recognizing the need for both growth and succession plans, to be in a position to operate at a market driven level. Fundamental to both of these plans is to ensure that the company has established systems, policies, procedures, and people, to create depth and capacity.

As obvious as this might sound, many founders simply build their companies around themselves, hiring staff to first address front line requirements, while the managers that follow are not developed to a point where they could fulfill their roles autonomously. All of these areas are critical components to building a sustainable, market driven business, one that could ultimately be transitioned to someone else (family members or otherwise).

In the case of family businesses, looking first to relatives to hold growth and succession roles is typical; however, in order to be effective, founders need to do more than simply hire those who are the closest to them. Rather, business leaders must first mentor future leaders with vision and understanding of the company at hand. This includes recognizing that one of the simplest and most effective things that a family business leader could do to engage family members is to talk to them about the company. Although this is a very straightforward concept, it is not always easy to do effectively.

Communicate Business Basics

Family business leaders have an opportunity to actively mentor their successors in a positive manner and consistency is an important component of doing so. This approach helps family members to be along for the ride in a way that is ongoing, constructive, and insightful, creating the foundation for a balanced understanding, where good decisions about what the future could hold can be made.

Begin the dialogue by providing family members with a basic understanding of the company, which could be approached by covering a range of topic areas, including:

- **Mission and vision.** What are the company's guiding principles and core values? What is the company's strategic and business plan, including goals, objectives, and estimated highlevel financial results? What is the anticipated future outlook for the company?

- **Industry trends and developments.** In what industry does the company reside? What are the key factors that impact it? What are some of the major trends and developments in the industry? How are areas such as products, services, and customer needs expected to evolve over time? Will the company still be of relevance in 10 years' time? In 20 years?

- **Main functions of the company.** What are the main products and/or services? What is the business model, in terms of how it "makes money"? Have its functions been reasonably consistent over time? What is expected to be the case in the future?

- **Markets and customers.** Who are the company's main customer groups? What are some of the important issues faced by customers? What needs in the marketplace does the company serve? What is the customer service philosophy?

- **Roles in the company.** What are the main functional areas in the business? What are the various roles? What qualifications and skills are required? What are the training and professional development requirements for advancement within the company?

- **Role in the community.** What is the business leader's vision for corporate citizenship within the community? What philanthropic efforts, volunteerism, and community accomplishments are undertaken by the company? How does its community role relate to its guiding principles and core values?

- **Future expansion plans.** Where is the company at today and what are some of the future plans (i.e., additional locations, new product lines, acquisitions, partnerships, etc.)? How could family members play a part in the company's future?

- **The difference between family business succession and family wealth succession.** There is a difference between the ongoing nurturing and growth of a company and stewardship of family wealth. Family members need to understand the difference and business leaders need to provide clarity around the issues of entitlement. Addressing this issue early, often, and in a consistent manner could help to manage expectations, increasing the likelihood of constructive family member involvement.

Sharing this basic information provides family members with a user-friendly introduction to the heart and soul of the company, its functions, customers, and the various roles within the enterprise. Family members will be in a better position to obtain a good understanding of the company's role within the community and what makes it successful, likely feeling some pride when important accomplishments occur, such as a new location or large contract.

Instead of regarding the company as a mysterious unknown that takes up space in their personal lives, family members will be more likely to feel that they are actually part of the business and team that makes it successful. They will also begin to understand that a business that operates well has the ability to provide for a family's economic needs, which is worthy of safeguarding and respect. Even more importantly, they might begin to see its future potential, and perhaps, one that could include their own unique and impactful role.

Understanding Roles and Responsibilities

Communicating key positions within the company is important, in terms of enabling family members to understand and relate to its human aspect, as well as visualizing themselves in a role. This area could be particularly powerful, as it represents the crossover point from a corporate entity to personal involvement.

Most of us could probably think of a situation where an ineffective son, daughter, or other relative is employed in a family business, with no meaningful position, knowledge, or ability to assist in its operation. Their sole credential is being a family member, and if we are left to wonder "what does he/she do all day?", just imagine what customers and other employees are thinking.

In these types of situations, there is often only a vague understanding of the "people who work for Mom", without any notion of the skills and experience that they bring to the company. Instead of a founder's children adopting the foregone conclusion that "I will work in the company when I grow up", they should, instead, have the necessary background information to take it upon themselves to acquire the knowledge and skills to qualify for and perform the role. It is at this point that a family member's potential contribution to the company could be purposefully explored.

In Vicky's case, her daughter, Ashley, might arrive at the conclusion that the design aspect of the company is too narrow to suit her interests, preferring instead to embark on a career with an interior design firm in order to achieve a greater degree of variety. Increased communication with Vicky might also reveal that attending client social events is far more work that it seems, casting a more realistic light on what working in the business actually entails.

Aidan, on the other hand, might actually be attracted to the management aspect of the company, and despite being less interested in the industry, see a good opportunity to gain practical finance and administration experience. In situations of this nature, family members could be coached in a manner that allows them to find their "fit", setting the stage for it to be pursued with clarity and focused planning.

By providing an understanding of the jobs that are part of the company and how each individual contributes to its success, family members could begin to gauge their level of interest, in terms of fulfilling a role, as well as understanding the skills and experience that are necessary for success. This provides business leaders with answers, as well as a tangible basis for dialogue with family members about the company and its future.

Setting Expectations and Options for Moving Forward

The extent to which realistic expectations are set, in terms of the necessary skills and knowledge to hold a key position within the company, could be the difference between a successful business and a failed enterprise—it could be this simple. In a rapidly changing and increasingly competitive economy, business leaders must spend more time than ever focused on marketplace challenges, increasing the importance of having clarity around internal issues; these matters simply cannot fill the day.

It is the responsibility of the family business leader to provide a clear indication of the necessary qualifications, particularly for senior level positions, including where specialized education and training are required, as well as any circumstances where simply being a family member is sufficient. The latter, although not recommended, might be acceptable for a Lifestyle Business; however, the former is a key requirement for building a Market Driven Business.

Since the goal of a Market Driven Business is to successfully compete based on the needs of the marketplace, each job must be staffed by a person, family member or otherwise, with the necessary skills and experience to perform the role well; anything less decreases the likelihood of good performance, thereby putting the company and the family's wealth at risk. It is also important to recognize that roles evolve and become increasingly complex as a company grows, thereby making ongoing professional development a given, in order to remain qualified.

Once this fact is communicated and consistently reinforced, it should have the effect of putting the company's requirements first, to the benefit of the family, as opposed to focusing on personal situations. Doing so is critical, as the goal is to create sustainable wealth for the family, and a company cannot be successful in doing so without a qualified management and staff group. Family members should also now be in a better position to decide as to whether they have an interest in taking on a day-to-day or passive role in the company.

Making the Decision

Given that family members have been engaged in a process to understand the company and their potential for involvement, which should ideally occur over a number of years, they should have the necessary information to make a decision. Although the outcome of this process provides answers and clarity, it could also be a sobering moment for business leaders.

Should family members not have an interest in working in the company, including in terms of succession, it is important for a business leader to receive this information sooner rather than later, so that alternate strategies could be developed. What could be helpful in doing so is to remember that the goal is to ensure that the company operates as a Market Driven Business, with appropriate depth to enable and support growth, especially at a senior level. If engagement of and ultimate succession to family members is not an option, business owners might find themselves in Vicky's tenuous situation—leading a successful company without a realistic succession plan.

Family members should be empowered to make their own decisions, as this decreases the likelihood of feeling pressured into a situation that is not of their own choosing. They should understand that a decision to take a day–to-day role in the company means that they would have a direct stake in the business's success or failure, input into decision making, and be compensated for their efforts, by way of salary, bonuses, ownership, or a combination thereof. This means that their compensation could be directly impacted by the company's performance, in good times and in bad, as well as in terms of their role in achieving it. This reality represents a "front row seat" and is very different from the peripheral involvement that might exist by simply being a family member.

There should also be clarity for those who decide to be passively involved, as they need to understand that this role does not include significant input or responsibility in terms of how the company is run or a salary or similar compensation. Rather, passive involvement might be limited to the potential to receive dividends and distributions, as seen fit by those who manage the business. This is an important and significance difference that must be understood.

Addressing Financial Issues

Once expectations for family member involvement in the company have been established and understood, business leaders need to address how to implement these roles, from a financial and structural perspective. This represents an area where assistance from professional advisors is critical.

In the case of potential ownership, the company might require a formal valuation and revision of its share structure and related agreements, to enable financial involvement by both active and passive family members on a fair and equitable basis. It is also important to recognize that business succession and family wealth succession are related, but should be considered separately. Possible approaches could include:

- **An estate freeze,** enabling actively involved family members to participate in the future growth of the company by owning shares.

- **Creating a new company or division,** that family member(s) could have the responsibility for developing and growing.

- **Structuring a transfer agreement,** where a portion of the company's shares could be moved to a family member(s) at some future point in time.

Arrangements of this nature could also involve structural components that are related to the role in the company that the family member holds, such as incentive plans to fund share purchases and/or professional development plans. All aspects of the arrangement, which should be developed with the assistance of a qualified advisor, have the benefit of focusing a family member's efforts on building the company and contributing to its financial results, as opposed to simply collecting a salary. This is important, as a Market Driven Business needs to have structures in place that emphasize generating success in the marketplace, as a means to maximize financial results, otherwise its performance level is unlikely to be sustainable over time.

A final note regarding family members who might opt not to be involved in the company on a day-to-day basis: Since everyone has and is entitled to their own goals and objectives in life, a decision to not join the business is understandable and should be treated as such. Instead of dwelling on disappointment and other negative feelings, Market Driven Business leaders should appreciate having this knowledge, focus on what is best for the company, and tell family members that their decision is respected. If the objective is to generate wealth, this is best achieved by having qualified, competent, and motivated individuals in the company, as opposed to reluctant family members.

However, in order to eliminate a "free ride" scenario, where uninvolved family members are given a token salary in exchange for little to no participation in the company, wealth should, instead, be transferred in other ways, such as dividends or distributions, perhaps, from a family trust. This approach is consistent with the objective of providing wealth to the family, without blurring the lines of day-to-day and passive involvement; it also levels the playing field.

Building a Succession Plan for a Market Driven Business

It is much easier to conduct succession planning for a company that is market driven, as compared to a Lifestyle Business, as emotion and family dynamics are effectively removed from the situation, leaving the focus on what is best for the enterprise. In addition, it is simply much easier to transition a viable business that is focused on market needs, as this type of company is more likely to be functioning well, of value, and sustainable over the long term. This is particularly important in the rapidly changing marketplace of today and what is expected to be the case for the foreseeable future.

The benefits of achieving market driven status have the potential to be enormous, including:

- **Clarity of Strategy.** Since the business leader has a thorough and realistic understanding where family members stand, in terms of active or passive involvement, it is possible to strategize for the future accordingly.

- **Transparency and Empowerment.** Family members have a good understanding of options for involvement and have been empowered to make a choice, thereby minimizing resentment and enabling them to take a leadership role in terms of the impact they could have on the business.

- **Clarity of Options.** Since the expectations and requirements for involvement are clear and consistent, family members understand what is required, in the event that they change their mind, and could take steps to gain the necessary knowledge and skills to join the company at some future point in time.

Any one of these areas will lighten a business leader's load, and when combined, the feeling should be such that a tremendous weight has been lifted. Too often, however, what could seem obvious tends to get lost in family dynamics, leading to less than desirable outcomes for everyone involved, including the business. In this scenario, however, the overall focus is on what is best for the company, a key requirement for building and managing a Market Driven Business. At the same time, knowledge, personal empowerment, and the ability to make choices should lead to respect for the company and the various roles that family members could opt to fulfill, as well as increased harmony around the dinner table.

SUMMARY: DEFUSING THE FAMILY BUSINESS TIME BOMB

Minefields

- Be consistent in setting expectations around the necessary skills and experience to hold a position in the company. Family members need to know that this area is not negotiable, otherwise the business will suffer.

- Do not pass judgment on active or passive involvement in the company. This will create "classes" within the family, inferring that one category is better than the other, causing friction and resentment. Respecting decisions made by others is important to maintaining family harmony; recognize that passive involvement is still involvement.

- If family members indicate that they do not wish to be actively involved with the business, do not delay in pursuing alternate growth and succession plans.

Tools

- Focus what is best for the business, as opposed to on family member situations. Remember that when a company's potential for success is at risk, the family's economic well-being and future are also in jeopardy.

- The cost of "carrying" an unqualified family member or one who is not willing to gain the necessary skills and experience comes at the expense of the family or business. Simply put, it is too much to ask.

- Give family members a reasonable amount of time to reach a decision, but don't delay. Business leaders need answers, so that an alternate growth and succession planning could occur where required.

- Using an independent business advisor could be helpful in developing a company's growth and succession plans. Advisors bring objectivity to the process and might be aware of individuals who could help take the company forward, in the event that family members do not have an interest in being actively involved.

YOUR MISSION: The Tricky Minefield of Family Involvement. Managing Starry Eyed Aspirations.

READY THINGS YOU NEED TO KNOW

- Growth and succession planning are key components of a Market Driven Business. Lifestyle Businesses should first focus on the areas that need to be addressed in order to operate at a market driven level and move forward from there.

- Do not assume that family members will join the company, be your successor, or operate in the same manner in which you do. All of these are examples of practicing imaginary succession.

- Family members benefit from receiving information about the company, how it functions, and the various roles and responsibilities. A good communication process helps family members to make an informed decision about their level of interest, in terms of working in the company on a day-to-day basis.

- The objective of engaging family members in a discussion process about the business should not be in an attempt to coerce them into taking an active role. The goal should be to provide information and assess their level of interest, creating the opportunity to reach a decision regarding day-to-day or passive involvement. Once made, this decision should provide guidance to business leaders as to whether or not alternate growth and succession planning steps are required.

- The focus should be on what is best for the company, with the goal of it operating as a Market Driven Business and generating wealth for the family. The best approach for generating success is to build a company of qualified, competent, motivated people, as opposed to one of reluctant family members. Companies need to be in a position to compete against the best in the marketplace in order to achieve long-term success.

SET QUESTIONS YOU NEED TO ASK

- Have I engaged family members in a communication process about the business?

- Do I make assumptions that family members would join the company?

- Do family members have a realistic understanding of the company and what involvement would entail?

- Have family members expressed an interest regarding involvement in the company?

- Have I communicated expectations regarding the necessary qualifications and experience to hold an active role in the company?

- Do I have a formal growth and succession plan for the company or have I been practicing imaginary succession?

THINGS YOU NEED TO DO

- Identify any gap areas and action items to bring resolution, as part of the transformation planning process.

- If the company has formal growth and succession plans, review to ensure that they are still current and have been developed with the objective of maintaining and growing a Market Driven Business, to create long-term wealth for the family.

- If you have not engaged family members in a meaningful dialogue about the business, it is time to start. Follow the guidelines of this chapter and develop an outline to start discussions with family members.

- If family members have indicated that they do not have an active interest in the company, it is time to move forward with alternate growth and succession planning.

DEFUSE DECISIONS YOU NEED TO MAKE

- Set expectations, in terms of the necessary qualifications for family members to join the company on a day-to-day basis. Determine if your approach is to staff each position with fully qualified and competent individuals to do the job, or if simply being a family member is sufficient qualification. Remember, marketplace leaders represent the direct competitors for any Market Driven Business, and if you want your company to be successful, especially in the new economy, having qualified people who can get the job done is a must.

- If family members have indicated an interest in joining the company on a day-to-day basis, determine if they possess the necessary skills and experience to successfully perform the role, or whether additional training or education is required. If so, this should be communicated to the family member.

✔ **Mission Accomplished:** Taking an active approach to introduce and educate family members about the company is a basic, but important, strategy for assessing their level of interest in being involved with its day-to-day operations. The goal should be to get an answer—to determine what the level of interest is—so that decisions could be made to guide family members into the right education and training opportunities, or to find and develop other options. Either way, the company's future is protected.

4

Bringing Performance Management to Life
How to Generate Results with Working Family Members

Brittany and her two older brothers work in her family's manufacturing business, founded many years ago by her grandfather, who has since retired. Brittany's father, Justin, manages the company, which has been highly successful for most of her life (Brittany is now 25). Both of her brothers pursued specialized education in the areas of engineering and computer technology, but Brittany never had much of an interest in school; instead, she found success playing competitive tennis. Now that those days are behind her, she spends most of her time with friends, a number of whom are from families with successful companies.

When Brittany joined the company almost two years ago, her father needed someone to help him manage the office. Justin was spending an increasing amount of time travelling and did not have the time to deal with office matters, believing that Brittany had the "people skills" to look after this area. Although she did not have a formal job title, Justin expected that she would take on increased responsibility as she became more acquainted with the business. Since Brittany's mother had encouraged her to find a job that was more consistent than the occasional tennis coaching lessons that she provided, working in the family business seemed ideal.

Despite this commitment, a friend of Brittany's asked her to partner in an upcoming doubles tournament. Brittany was spending more time practicing and less time in the office, and while staff members were reluctant to say anything to Justin, they were definitely feeling pressure from the lack of direction. They did not find her to be particularly helpful anyway, given that she did not have a background in accounting or management, which left staff members to do the best they could to resolve issues on their own.

Kiki, the company's accounting manager, was becoming increasingly frustrated from being "supervised" by someone who knew far less about the company than she did and started looking for employment elsewhere. Kiki was an excellent staff member who had been with the company for six years and would have been the logical choice to be promoted to oversee the office. She realized that unless Justin took steps to address Brittany's job performance, she was in a hopeless situation.

THE ISSUES

How many times have you heard this story? A family business employs a relative who does not have the necessary skills to perform the largely undefined role that they were given, to the detriment of staff members, customers, and the company itself. Staff members are reluctant to raise the issue with the business leader and either find a way to cope with the situation or seek alternate employment. The business leader is either unaware of the problem or has no idea how to correct the situation, given that it involves disciplining (or perhaps firing!) a family member. In the end, the company loses, as talented staff members, customers, and even potential employees look elsewhere to have their business and/or employment needs fulfilled. And of course, the family's wealth ultimately suffers when the company is negatively impacted in the marketplace. There might have been times when this situation was somewhat survivable, but given the new economy of increased customer expectations and competitive offerings, it is simply not sustainable.

What is unfortunate is that many business leaders do not fully appreciate just how significant of a problem this scenario is, one that multiplies with each poorly managed or unqualified hire. Consider the following negative impacts on a company, due to the "mis-employment" of a family member.

- **Staff members who are performing at an *average* level.** Those who meet the basic expectations of their role would not typically realize their potential and perform at a higher level in situations where the company accepts less than average job performance from others (family members or otherwise). Why is this the case? Simply because it sends a message that it is acceptable to perform below what is ideally required, and when given the choice, these employees tend to follow the norm. This relatively low level of performance is not sufficient to enable a company to successfully compete in the marketplace, at the level of a Market Driven Business, which represents an ultimate cost to the organization. Companies that fall into this category do not represent marketplace leaders and face the risk of being displaced by better managed competitors.

- **Staff members who are performing at an *above average* level.** A company's "stars" might become unmotivated to continue to perform at a high level when they see less than average performance being accepted. This situation might surprise some people, as high achievers are often regarded as operating at a strong level of performance, regardless of their environment. This is not a given, and in fact, this type of situation could be extremely frustrating for above-average performers, who initially tend to trust that the company will take steps to correct what is an obvious imbalance that limits the business from functioning at its best.

If this does not occur, above average performers tend to feel that their efforts are not appreciated or are taken for granted, resulting in either a decrease in their level of performance and engagement, to an average level (thereby creating their own sense of fairness), or looking for opportunities outside of the company. Either way, these are the type of individuals that companies do not want to lose, and their departure or diminished performance represents a significant cost to the business.

If you are not convinced that this actually happens, think about the last time that a company's business leader was shocked by the resignation of their "star" employee, something that they never would have expected. The truth is: it happens all the time, strong performers have more employment options than others, and this type of scenario could be what triggers a move.

- **Potential staff members.** When the company attempts to hire individuals to replace those who have left, they might find it more difficult to do so than anticipated. Potential staff members might become aware that if they join the company, they would be reporting to a less than competent family member, and high performing candidates, in particular, tend to look for a better arrangement. It is also not unusual for this type of information to be discussed within the business community, including amongst recruiters, candidates, and those who have had dealings with the company. Once this type of reputation becomes established, it could be difficult to overcome, with the company being labelled as a "weak link" or unhealthy work environment. As a result, the company is left with a pool of average to weak candidates from which they could draw, or is unable to fill positions at all. Once a company is on this path, the likelihood of good performance or generating value is remote, at best.

- **Customers.** Customers look to suppliers and service providers to fulfill their needs in a competent, reliable, and reasonably priced manner, and no one wants to deal with a company that cannot or will not meet their requirements. If a company does not have a competent management and staff group, they face the very real risk of losing customers to competitors that are in a better position to meet marketplace needs. This type of situation represents a clear loss of wealth and value creation opportunities for the company and the family, which only gets worse until corrected. Failing to do so raises the likelihood that stories of poor customer service and unmet needs will spread throughout the marketplace, which is especially easy to do in today's digital world.

The Bottom Line: Family businesses cannot afford to "carry" anyone who isn't getting the job done; be it a function of a lack of skills, experience, training, or attitude. This situation is especially problematic when the culprit is a family member, as associated shortfalls are damaging not only to their own livelihood, but also to that of their relatives. Business leaders are responsible for setting and maintaining the standard so that this type of situation never occurs, otherwise the company could become seriously diminished and unable to recover.

THE SOLUTIONS

You might think that Brittany is solely to blame for this situation; however, she is only part of the problem. Justin failed to do a number of things to put Brittany in a position where she had a reasonable chance of being successful, and then did not address the matter when it became truly unacceptable.

What steps could Justin have taken to prevent this scenario from occurring? To begin, business leaders must:

- Engage family members in a communication process about the company as an entity;

- Set clear and consistent expectations, in terms of skills, education requirements, experience, and performance guidelines to qualify for and perform the role; and

- Provide family members with an opportunity to reach a decision regarding their level of interest in holding an active role in the company

While we do not know if Justin engaged his children in a communication process about the company, or if they were empowered to select an active or passive role, there is one important consideration that is apparent:

Justin did not set clear and consistent expectations for Brittany's involvement in the company. This could be drawn from the scenario, given that Brittany: (i) does not have any formal education or experience to manage the office, which is clearly a shortfall; and (ii) is poorly equipped to manage an office of administrative and accounting staff members, given her lack of relevant education and experience. Justin's failure to set the expectation that specific skills, education, and experience are required to successfully perform this type of role put Brittany at a disadvantage from the start.

This situation could have been avoided by following the guidelines that are discussed in Chapter 3, particularly in terms of providing clear and consistent expectations for the requirements of the job. In the case of a poorly performing family member, business leaders need to first look to their own behavior and ask "Did the expectations that I set (or failed to set) create this situation? Am I the one who is at fault?" If the answer is yes, immediate steps should be taken to ensure that this type of behavior is not repeated and any unacceptable situations that have occurred as a result (such as in Brittany's case) are resolved.

Having said that, it is important that, once this has been done, business leaders must not fall into a pattern of self-blame and guilt, as doing so detracts from family members being accountable for their own shortfalls. This tendency is something that must be carefully monitored, as in moments of weakness, it is easy for a business leader to blame themselves. They also need to understand that what might have started out as a seemingly harmless "internal family matter" has the potential to put a company in significant jeopardy.

There are a number of important areas that should be addressed in order to avoid problem areas and put the company in a better position, when it comes to employing family members. Doing so raises the likelihood that business leaders will be well situated to generate meaningful results with family members over the long term.

Employment Contracts and Policies

It is important for family members to recognize that joining any company is a serious undertaking; this includes the family business. This consideration is one that should not be taken lightly, as people sometimes view working in their family's company as a right, hobby, or fallback position, as compared to "real world" employment. However, these ideas might come to pass, it is critical that business leaders acquaint family members with the commercial realities of being actively involved in the company, from the very beginning.

As with any employee, family members should be a party to a contract that formally defines their role with the company, as well as the related terms, conditions, and arrangements. An employment contract, or similar document, is useful for communicating all of this information to staff members, so that they understand the role and associated obligations of both the individual and the company. A qualified human resources professional or legal advisor could assist in preparing employment contracts and guidelines for implementation.

Before arriving at a quick conclusion along the lines of "this sounds like too much work" or "that could be done later", it is important to recognize that this type of thinking represents a dangerous pitfall. Companies could unexpectedly find themselves in a situation where staff members are quickly hired (relatives or otherwise) to support short term demand or bona fide growth, without taking the time to "do the paperwork". Months could pass, and as circumstances evolve, the situation might look quite different than it did when the person commenced employment, leading to a need to terminate or re-assign staff members. In the absence of a professionally drafted employment agreement, companies could find themselves facing legal problems due to misunderstandings or difficulty in getting staff members to sign an agreement that should have been dealt with months ago. These types of situations tend to create costly and time-consuming problems for business leaders that could have been easily avoided.

Growing companies tend to face challenges in terms of implementing appropriate documentation, policies, procedures, and performance management tools in a manner that provides the necessary structure to support future growth. Implementation of employment contracts and other human resources policies not only protects the business, it also integrates a professional management approach into the company, including for the engagement of family members. It is important to remember that these areas represent basic requirements for taking a Lifestyle Business to the level of a Market Driven Business.

Reasonable Compensation for the Job Performed

The amount of compensation for a position should be based on the value that the job brings to the company, period. This could be assessed by considering factors such as the degree of complexity and risk associated with the tasks and responsibilities of the job, as well as the level of expertise, knowledge, and education or training required to hold the position. This simple approach could bring clarity to an area where business leaders tend to struggle.

In order to understand a company's overall compensation structure, salary ranges should be developed for each position in the organizational chart. This process allows a business leader to review the compensation level for all roles, in terms of both reasonableness and in the context of the company as a whole. It is this concept of "context" that decreases the likelihood of outlier situations, where a position's compensation is either too high or too low.

Salary ranges provide room for an individual's earnings to progress as they become more proficient at performing the job, as well as some flexibility to compensate for any specific qualifications that an individual might hold. When salary ranges are developed, consideration should also be given to comparable earnings levels of similar jobs in the marketplace, to ensure that the level of compensation is sufficient to attract qualified candidates. These are areas where qualified human resources advisors could be of assistance.

From a compensation perspective, it is not appropriate to pay an individual at a level above the relative worth of a job, and this could be a particularly tempting situation when dealing with family members. If an appropriate and consistent compensation strategy is not applied across all jobs in the company, the outcome is that certain positions would be "skewed" from the norm, solely because they are held by family members (remember those outliers?). This is not an equitable arrangement, nor is it helpful for assisting family members with obtaining a realistic understanding of what the role is actually worth to the company. It is also not helpful in situations where a job is no longer held by a family member and someone else is being assigned to the role.

Consider the following approach to compensate family members:

- First, compensate family members for the **position that they hold in the company.** Their compensation level in this regard should be consistent with a reasonable salary range for the position, as well as the family member's skills and qualifications.

- Next, compensate family members for their **level of performance,** in terms of the how well they perform the job, as compared to established evaluation criteria (see the Regular and Constructive Performance Feedback section below). This compensation could be provided in the form of bonuses, profit sharing, or other items, and should be determined based on the level of performance that is achieved.

Performance-based compensation could be divided into short-term or annual (i.e., bonuses, profit sharing, etc.) and long-term (i.e., stock options, etc.) components, with the latter providing targets for an individual to work towards over a period of greater than one year. This approach rewards family members for performance in the current year, while encouraging them to focus on what they could achieve over the next few years.

- Finally, family members might **hold shares in the company or receive dividends** or other distributions based on their role in the family, or agreements to take over the business at some point in the future. This category of compensation is separate from that of the job they hold, which typically includes salary, performance-based compensation, and perks and benefits.

Addressing compensation *can be this simple,* putting an end to confusion, ad hoc approaches, and a perceived lack of fairness. It also helps to focus family members on what is important, defusing problems before they start.

Structuring compensation using this approach provides family members with a clear understanding, in terms of the amounts and entitlements that pertain to holding and successfully performing a job, while keeping ownership and/or investment related earnings separate. It also helps to level the playing field between family and non-family members, recognizing that everyone in the company has both responsibilities and rewards that are directly related to holding a position. In addition, a clear indication of the fair value of the position is established, something that is particularly important for family members to understand (and remember).

Clearly Defined Job Responsibilities

The fact that Brittany joined the company without a formal job title and with the expectation that she would take on increased responsibility as she became more familiar with the business represents Strike Two. She was only given vague direction, in terms of being responsible for overseeing the office, with no supervision or mentorship from her father of what was required in the role and how to perform it. The fact that Justin was often away from the office did not help matters.

All positions should have a written job description that clearly outlines the main responsibilities of the role. Job descriptions should indicate whether the position has a lead, shared, or supporting responsibility for each task, as well as the necessary skills, experience, and education to hold the role. Since a job description provides a clear indication of what the role entails, it is essentially a precursor for performance evaluation, which is discussed in the next section.

Job descriptions also provide clarity of how the various roles within the organization relate to one another and which position is responsible for which tasks. This is particularly important, in terms of resolving disputes pertaining to "who does what", as well as for identifying any areas that have not been assigned. Experienced business leaders recognize that these tend to be common areas of dispute, in situations where roles have not been well defined, but also in the case of growth companies, where job descriptions have fallen behind front-line reality.

Job descriptions also include information about the compensation range for the position, as well as reporting relationships with other roles in the organization. This information is useful in helping staff members to understand possible promotion and advancement opportunities, setting the stage for career planning. This could be particularly helpful for demonstrating to family members that advancement typically requires work experience and professional development, as opposed to simply occurring with time.

Recruitment is another area where job descriptions are useful, as they indicate the necessary level of education, skills, experience, and compensation for the role, facilitating selection of appropriate candidates, while screening out those who do not qualify. Templates and guidelines for developing job descriptions are readily available in human resources publications, from a qualified business advisor, and online. Be sure to utilize a format that fits well with your company.

One of the things that a business leader might notice when first attempting to develop job descriptions is that some of the information tends to come very easily, while other areas require a fair amount of thought. This is particularly true when determining exactly how some functions that are shared by various positions are addressed, as well as identifying the role that is the most appropriate to perform a given task. A key risk to keep in mind is that if tasks are not assigned to the appropriate role, it could impact the company's performance (and fall, by default, to the wrong place). This situation could be attributed to various reasons, however, one that is abundantly clear is the problems that arise due to poorly organized workflow, which does not facilitate efficient operation, regardless of the level of talent and ability of a company's staff members. "Stars" in a poor system can have difficulty getting to a good result.

If you are confused just thinking about this area, imagine how difficult it is for a company's staff members to function well in the absence of this valuable information. Defining roles and responsibilities, in a lot of ways, represents Job #1, and if a company's staff members are not performing well, "wasting time", or asking too many "annoying questions", business leaders often have no one to blame but themselves.

Regular and Constructive Performance Feedback

Providing meaningful and timely feedback on staff member performance is an important aspect of any company that strives to compete successfully in the marketplace. A Market Driven Business must always put its best foot forward and an important component of doing so is ensuring that all jobs within the company are being performed well. This should be the case in a range of circumstances: whether the company's workload is busy or slow, regardless of which staff members are "at the wheel", and so on.

When a company is consistently guided by what needs to be done in order to be successful in the marketplace, it does not matter if the position is held by a family member or someone else. What matters is that the job is being performed effectively, otherwise the business, and ultimately the family, suffers.

Performance feedback could include both informal and formal aspects. Informal performance feedback is conducted on an ongoing basis and could be as simple as a manager congratulating a staff member for a particular job task or situation that was performed well, such as resolving a customer problem. Conversely, when a staff member has difficulty with a particular situation, it is most effectively addressed at that point in time, as the opportunity exists to obtain an immediate understanding of what did not go well and how it could be better addressed in the future.

Informal performance feedback allows staff members to know where they stand at any point in time, in terms of job performance, and takes the dangerous "surprise" element out of performance evaluation. People also take comfort in knowing that if there is a problem, it will be brought to their attention on a timely and constructive basis, instead of being unfairly stockpiled for confrontation at some future point in time. This should clearly demonstrate the significant difference that business leaders could make, simply by how they deliver feedback.

Performance feedback of a formal nature usually involves a structured evaluation, conducted at least once per year (many companies have performance evaluation sessions twice per year). This type of evaluation is based on rating a staff member's performance of job tasks and responsibilities, by utilizing predetermined criteria. A job description should provide the basis for the areas in which performance is evaluated, since it includes a list of tasks and responsibilities that comprise the role. This approach allows staff members to clearly understand the tasks and responsibilities upon which they are being evaluated, providing the important linkage between areas of responsibility and job performance. If this information is properly conveyed, there should not be any surprises in terms of how staff performance is measured.

A typical evaluation approach is to score performance in each area on a numeric scale (i.e., a scale of 1 to 5, for example), supported by written comments that provide further explanation. The combination of numeric ranking and qualitative comments provides staff members with tangible feedback, as well as some context for the evaluation. This type of approach requires the evaluator to consider their assessment in a structured and thorough manner, and it also minimizes the likelihood of evaluations that lack substance.

As an example, a performance evaluation scale could have the following categories:

5. Consistently exceeds the requirements of the position in this area; staff member is ready to take on more senior tasks/responsibilities

4. Generally, exceeds the requirements of the position in this area; staff member performs at an above average level

3. Meets the requirements of the position in this area; staff member performs at an average level

2. Does not consistently meet the requirements of the position in this area; has a basic understanding, but is not performing at a satisfactory level

1. Does not meet the requirements of the position in this area

A performance evaluation should include an action plan of items to be achieved within a specified period of time. An action plan could be developed for those who require improvement, as well as for high performing staff members, setting targets for enhanced areas of responsibility and promotion. It is important that action plans have a limited number of tasks, allowing for focused improvement and completion.

Although performance feedback involves an assessment of how well an individual is performing, it need not be an overly "personal" nature. Business leaders should instead consider the needs to the company and what is required to achieve performance at a market driven level, as opposed to dwelling on personal circumstances. Put another way, since it is a reasonable expectation that most people do not come to work to be an ineffective staff member, the goal should be to address job performance constructively and determine how improvements could be made. Strategies might involve additional training, education, or perhaps, assignment to another role in the company. Although not all performance issues can be successfully resolved, a well-defined feedback program has the ability to proactively address many issues, to the benefit of the company and everyone involved.

Addressing Training and Professional Development Requirements

It is important to recognize that most successful companies are learning organizations. This means that there is a culture and requirement for all staff members to gain knowledge and update their skills on a continuous basis, from the business leader to the most junior roles in the company. Ongoing training and professional development could take a variety of formats, including online learning, seminars, conferences, in-house training sessions, courses, and professional designations.

Opportunities exist for companies to cover fees associated with staff member training and professional development and deduct the costs for income tax purposes; however, better outcomes are likely when this is done upon successful completion of the session. Ongoing professional development programs paid for by an employer could be a useful recruitment tool for attracting above-average performers, as this type of individual often has a high degree of interest in learning and advancement opportunities.

As previously mentioned, formal performance evaluations should include an action plan of items for achievement by a specified point in time. Identifying developmental requirements, such as completing a recognized designation in order to be considered for promotion opportunities, could be useful for maintaining a high level of job performance and the basis for implementing a company-wide professional development program. This approach could also be used in instances of below average performance, as additional training and knowledge typically provide the necessary tools for improvement, leaving the rest to the individual. Business leaders should also be able to draw some comfort from having taken the necessary steps to provide each staff member with the opportunity to perform at an acceptable level, with the best interest of the company in mind. Whether or not they take the next step is up to them, which could provide a refreshing degree of certainty either way.

Transfer and Termination

Unfortunately, not all hiring decisions are successful, and this could be the case for both employees and family members. A Market Driven Business is characterized by an environment that focuses on competing successfully in the marketplace, which requires above-average performance within the company; anything less does not support market leadership. From a human resources perspective, this includes implementing, at a minimum, job descriptions, regular and constructive performance feedback, and a training and professional development program. Doing so raises the likelihood of successful staffing decisions and job performance; however, it will not eliminate every problem.

When it comes to hiring family members, it is absolutely critical that the basis for termination be discussed when the person joins the company, as well as considering how it would play out, both in terms of the business and family environment. This planning component is integral to all recruitment situations, but one that could be particularly important in the context of family life.

Business leaders need to take immediate and decisive steps when family members are not a fit for the role or the company. When this moment is reached, it is typically not without a significant amount of deliberation and angst, which generally bring little in avoiding the ultimate outcome. Business leaders could struggle with these decisions for years, but should be guided by the knowledge that without taking steps to protect the company and resolve the situation, they severely limit the likelihood of a positive outcome.

At this point in time, there is a realization that additional training or professional development are not sufficient to address the issue. Accordingly, options for resolution could involve:

- Moving the individual to another position or department within the company, for which they are better suited; or

- Terminating the employment relationship

A transfer should not occur to simply "move the problem"; rather, it should only be done in situations where there is a high likelihood that the individual would be successful in the new position. This should be thoroughly considered by way of an assessment process, including reviewing the job description, training needs, and professional development requirements with the family member to ensure that there is a fit with their qualifications and ability. It is also important to consider attitude related issues, including determining whether or not there is a bona fide willingness to make the change. This type of process could be conducted with the assistance of a qualified human resources professional or business advisor.

When there are no other reasonable options, unacceptable job performance should never be tolerated by a company, whether an employee or family member is involved. Termination of the employment relationship should occur, utilizing the best practices for doing so, including the following:

- Ensure that formal performance evaluations and incidences of unacceptable performance/behavior, if applicable, are documented in writing.

- If attempts to improve job performance, such as coaching, training, and professional development are not successful, termination should occur on a timely basis.

- The individual's direct supervisor/manager should typically conduct the termination in a meeting that is specifically set for this purpose.

- It is helpful for the meeting to be attended by a qualified human resources professional, either employed by the company or an external advisor, to address the individual's administrative and personal requirements after the manager has completed the termination and left the meeting.

- A letter confirming the termination and related arrangements should be provided to the departing staff member during the meeting. Preparation of termination letters should be conducted by a qualified human resources professional or legal advisor.

- Once the termination has been completed, the company's staff members should be immediately informed of its occurrence, with the emphasis being on how responsibilities would be transitioned or fulfilled. It is helpful to assure staff members that the focus is on going forward, in a positive and constructive manner.

- Once an individual has been terminated, they should be allowed to briefly collect their personal effects and then leave the premises.

- Severance packages should be structured in accordance with appropriate standards, that reflect legal and regulatory requirements and are consistently applied.

- A career coaching service provided by a qualified human resources firm could be helpful, in terms of moving the terminated staff member forward (i.e., resume preparation, counselling, networking, access to employment opportunities, etc.)

It is always a good idea to consult qualified advisors to address any specific questions or needs, in advance of conducting a termination. The focus should always be on what is in the best interest of the company and the people who work in it, which means creating and maintaining an effective management and staff group, family members or otherwise. At the same time, departing employees should be treated with compassion and respect, while being firm in terms of the reality of the situation.

It might be intimidating to think about the prospect of terminating a family member, but instead, consider all of the things that could have been done to avoid reaching this difficult point in time, including:

- Engaging family members in a communication process about the business, in terms of its key functions, customers, and roles.

- Setting clear and consistent expectations in terms of required skills, knowledge, and experience level to hold a particular position.

- Allowing family members to make an informed decision as to whether they wish to take an active or passive role in the business.

- Using employment contracts for all staff members, outlining the role, terms and conditions, compensation, and obligations of both the individual and the company.

- Providing clear responsibilities for the role, by way of a job description that includes tasks, obligations, qualifications, relationship to other positions in the company, and compensation arrangements.

- Providing regular and constructive performance feedback, particularly in terms of areas that require improvement and an action plan for ongoing development.

- Creating a learning environment, through training and professional development to address performance shortfalls and provide the necessary knowledge for promotion, advancement, and new experiences.

When a business leader provides all of the necessary support and guidance to enable a family member to make a good decision about their level of involvement with the company and identifies a role that is well-suited to their skills and interests, they have created a winning situation. Anything less is simply not fair to the company, reinforcing the fact that the best place for a low-performing family member is on the sideline in a passive role.

SUMMARY: DEFUSING THE FAMILY BUSINESS TIME BOMB

Minefields

- If a staff member is performing poorly, do not "look the other way" and hope that improvements will happen with time. The above average performers in the company are counting on you to resolve the situation, now.

- Do not consider human resources management to be a "soft" skill area that is of little importance. Staff members often represent a company's largest expense, which should be viewed as its most significant investment and resource. Isn't this something that is worth managing?

Tools

- Staff members who are well-directed, trained, and motivated typically perform well. An effective staff and management group is a valuable resource for any business.

- It is important to be consistent in terms of implementing and maintaining human resources policies and procedures. Staff members need to know that these requirements are applicable to everyone, all of the time.

- Investing the time and effort to implement appropriate documentation, policies, and procedures should be viewed as an investment in your company. Not only will the business operate more effectively with established guidelines and practices, it will also be better protected when problems arise. This type of framework also increases the value of a company and is integral to the professional management approach that is exemplified by a Market Driven Business.

- No customer wants to deal with a company that cannot or will not meet their needs. Market leaders strive to consistently exceed customer expectations, and this is only possible with a competent and professional staff and management group.

YOUR MISSION: Bringing Performance Management to Life. How to Generate Results with Working Family Members.

`READY` THINGS YOU NEED TO KNOW

- If a family member is performing poorly in a job, they might not be solely to blame for the situation. It is possible that consistent expectations, in terms of the necessary qualifications and requirements to hold a position, were not set by the business leader.

- Customers will not continue to be loyal to a company in times of below average performance. In these situations, it is likely that the better performers in the marketplace (i.e., the Market Driven Businesses) would be in a position to gain customers.

- It is possible to create an environment for good job performance and business leaders should do so for all roles in the company. Clear expectations, in terms of roles and responsibilities, compensation, performance feedback, training and professional development, and opportunities for advancement could empower all staff members, family or otherwise, to be successful.

`SET` QUESTIONS YOU NEED TO ASK

- Have clear and consistent expectations been provided to family members, in terms of the qualifications and requirements for roles in the company?

- Have guidance and mentorship been provided to help family members become acquainted with the company and their role?

- Does the company have employment contracts for all staff members?

- Does the company provide clear information, in terms of the tasks, responsibilities, and qualifications for each position, by way of job descriptions?

- Does the company provide regular performance feedback, including evaluation and action planning for improvement?

- Does the company have a learning culture, in terms of promoting training and professional development opportunities and requirements?

- Are family members compensated at a level that is reasonable for the position that they hold?
- In the case of staff members that are not performing well, have steps been taken to address the situation?

THINGS YOU NEED TO DO

- Identify any gap areas and action items to bring resolution, as part of the transformation planning process.
- Review the company's existing human resources systems and policies and take steps to improve this functional area. Doing so is useful for all family businesses and is an important component of moving to a market driven level.
- Schedule a meeting with a qualified human resources professional to discuss how your company is currently performing. Inquire as to the types of services that they provide and what steps should be taken to improve the human resources function in your business.
- If there are members of the company who are not performing as required, action must be taken to resolve the situation. Waiting or hoping for circumstances to change is not effective and could do harm to the business.

`DEFUSE` DECISIONS YOU NEED TO MAKE

- Identify any situations where family members who are actively involved in the company are not adequately fulfilling their role and determine how the matter should be resolved.
- Determine whether to engage a qualified human resources professional to assist with implementing the areas discussed in this chapter or if your company is large enough to warrant a full-time human resources manager.
- If your company currently has a human resources staff member or department, but is not adequately addressing the areas outlined in this chapter, determine what steps should be taken to resolve the situation.

✔ **Mission Accompished:** Recognizing that successful competitors in the marketplace (those who operate at a market driven level) would not employ your own poorly performing family member puts it all into perspective. If the individual is not sufficiently qualified to be an employee in their company, why would you want them in your business?

5

Engaging Non-Family Members

How to Ensure that Valuable Resources Stay, Instead of Get Away

Twin sisters Sydney and Sally are architects. They have owned and managed an architectural firm that completes residential and commercial projects for the past five years. When they started the company, they found themselves with an increasing number of large commercial projects, while home renovation clients represented a smaller portion of their work. This meant that Sydney and her three staff members had lots to do, while Sally and her team, on the residential side of the business, had a steady, but less chaotic workload.

Sydney has been backlogged with projects for months and does not have enough staff members with senior level experience. She would like to hire an architect with project experience to provide more capacity, but at the same time, is unsure what impact recent economic conditions might have on her workload. Sally has suggested that since this new role would be senior to the rest of the staff, it should be held by a family member. Their niece, Lilly, is currently studying interior design and works part-time in the company. Lilly will graduate in just over a year, and although she has been working mostly in the residential side of the business, Sally believes that she would be a good candidate to help Sydney with her busy workload.

Sydney is not convinced. Although promoting Lilly could provide a quick solution, she is concerned about her lack of work experience and architectural skills and does not believe that she would be senior enough to competently take on the role at this point. But, Sydney cannot help but wonder, would hiring an external person be "de-motivating" to Lilly, who with the proper training and experience, could be a good candidate for the position in a few years? On the other hand, if she hired someone from outside of the family, what type of compensation structure would be required? Would they expect an ownership position in the company? Looking at the pile of drawings strewn across her desk, Sydney takes a sip of her latte and considers her next steps.

THE ISSUES

Sydney and Sally need to quickly resolve their work backlog in order to meet the needs and expectations of their clients. Given the nature of their business, the work must be done properly and is best performed by those with specialized education, experience, and professional designations. Lilly might possess some of the necessary requirements, but likely not all, and is at least a few years away from being a strong candidate for the role.

It might seem obvious that Sydney and Sally should look to a qualified non-family member for the role they plan to create, but in many family businesses, the temptation could be to give the position to a relative, whose qualifications are "close enough", to achieve a quick solution and maintain familial harmony. This could represent a significant mistake, regardless of the type of company.

What happens when a family business grows to a point where more specialized resources are required? Unless the business leader has been setting expectations and guiding family members towards obtaining the necessary education and experience to hold key positions, the company might have to look to other options, including hiring qualified non-family members to assume these important roles. Failing to do so limits the opportunity of a company to grow, in terms of its knowledge base and capability, which could put it in a weaker position in the competitive marketplace, as well as in facing the unique challenges that the new economy presents.

Bringing on non-family members to hold key positions could backfire, however, unless they are properly integrated into the company. The business environment must be such that non-family members feel welcome, treated fairly, and that the opportunity truly exists for advancement to more senior positions, as opposed to watching priority being given to family members, regardless of whether they possess the necessary qualifications. These talented individuals will leave to pursue other opportunities if this is the case, thereby limiting the growth and potential of the company, to the detriment of the family.

Consider the following scenarios:

- For business leaders who have specialized training, as in the case of Sydney and Sally, qualified non-family members represent a useful resource that could take on some of the excess workload in key areas. This would allow their company to do more, immediately.

- For business leaders who do not have specialized training, it is important to hire non-family members with expertise to expand the company's technical ability and product/service offerings. This allows the business to do new things today and improve its competitive position in the marketplace for better results tomorrow. However, if not properly managed, complications could (and do) arise, such as the following:

○ Depending on the personality and attributes of the business leader, they might begin to feel overshadowed or threatened by an employee who has more knowledge than they do. As petty as this situation might sound, it is one that happens *far more often* than would be expected.

○ Based on the situation at hand, a non-family staff member might feel isolated in a company where there are no senior leaders from whom they could learn, due to the lack of specialized knowledge at the top of the organization.

○ A non-family staff member might also feel uncomfortable if the rationale for their joining the business has not been explained to family who work in the company, which could lead to resentment, given that there is an external person in the role. This type of environment could become untenable for the talented resource who has been brought in to help the family grow its business, resulting in their departure.

• Family members who do not have the skills and experience to hold a particular position might also be dissatisfied, if the rationale for hiring a qualified external person was not properly explained or implemented. If family members do not have specialized expertise, they might not appreciate the specific job requirements and be of the view that they themselves are sufficiently qualified for the role. This type of situation could result in everything from resentment of the non-family member, to undermining, and even worse, as facts tend to become irrelevant once the situation has been mishandled. This type of scenario has the potential to do significant damage a company, not to mention family relationships.

The real danger is that once a company gets a reputation for being a "closed shop" to non-family members, even if and when they come to their senses, it might be too late to attract high quality resources. This scenario is not theoretical; rather, **it is one that is very real.**

The Bottom Line: Business leaders must have a strategy for hiring qualified non-family members to bring new skills and expertise to the company. This is particularly important in the case of Market Driven Businesses, requiring a well qualified individual in every position, family member or otherwise. In order to get there, developing a strategy and planning for implementation are critical.

THE SOLUTIONS

Creating an environment where qualified non-family members could make a meaningful contribution to the business, thereby increasing the wealth of the family, must be mindful of both the needs of the organization and the individual. A company needs to be in a position to truly welcome others, recognizing that they represent an opportunity to bring tremendous knowledge and ability, however, their needs could be unique, and as long as they are within reason, it is important that they be respected. Non-family members have both personal and professional needs, in terms of a welcoming environment and a sense of belonging, as well as matters such as reasonable compensation, decision-making ability, access to professional development, and advancement opportunities.

When these needs are met, engaging external resources could be a viable strategy, raising the likelihood of successfully competing in the marketplace and generating family wealth. Conversely, if the situation is not fully addressed, the company is at significant risk of losing these talented staff members. Before reading any further, take a moment to think about what this means. The reason for engaging talented people is to improve a company, in terms of its performance, market position, long term viability, and financial results. When non-family members who have the ability to make this happen walk out the door, they take this potential with them. This represents a loss of what could be substantial value, period.

Qualified non-family members could supplement the business leader role(s) by taking over some of the workload or providing skills and expertise that are not currently held by the company. This, in turn, creates an opportunity to train and develop others and contributes to the powerful concept of a learning organization. It could also represent an opportunity for assuming the leadership role at some future point in time.

Let's consider some of the key components that must be addressed to successfully integrate qualified non-family members into a company, especially at a senior level.

Reinforce the Need for Specialized Skills and Experience

As discussed in Chapter 3, a Market Driven Business needs specific skills and experience in order to be successful. If family members are taught that focusing on what is best for the company is the most appropriate approach for generating wealth, as opposed to giving priority to personal situations, this will be obvious to them. If not, it could be very difficult to make progress.

Bringing on a qualified non-family member is one approach that could be used to integrate specialized expertise into a family business. Another approach is to utilize a non-family member as an interim resource, as perhaps in the case of Lilly, where a relative is not quite ready to take on a role. This type of staged approach could meet the needs of an external person who is looking for a senior level engagement for a limited period of time, perhaps just prior to retirement, and could also represent a mentorship opportunity for a newly qualified family member to transition into the job. This approach could also be an attractive stepping stone for qualified individuals who are looking to build their career experience.

The key is to set expectations for family members and remind them to focus first on the needs of the company. This could be as simple as reinforcing that having the right expertise to generate success is what is important, regardless of the source. Once the stage has been set, utilizing this approach could be beneficial well into the future.

Remind Family Members of Their Choice

Once family members have been engaged in a communication process that sets consistent expectations for the requirements and qualifications to join the company, they should be empowered to decide whether they wish to be actively or passively involved. If they choose to be actively involved, this must be contingent upon achieving the necessary qualifications to perform the particular job. Family members must arrive at a deliberate choice, qualify for the role, and make a formal commitment to fulfil the associated responsibilities.

This is very important and represents a baseline requirement that must be remembered when the time comes for succession planning in a family business. Those who had to qualify, commit, and then actively participate in building the company need to be acknowledged accordingly throughout this process. If they are successful in their role and any necessary advancement, this should be considered when the time comes for succession of the leadership role, assuming that both parties have an interest making this transition and arriving at a suitable arrangement to do so.

In the event that a company requires specialized expertise, family members should realize that it is within their control to pursue the necessary education and/or training to become a candidate for the role. They should also recognize that it is up to the business leader to identify the individual that is best suited for the position, family member or otherwise, with the guiding objective being the best interest of the company.

When this approach is consistently utilized, family members should recognize that a qualified non-family member is not being "imposed" upon them; rather, the situation should be viewed as a solution to ensure the ongoing capability and competitiveness of the business, with their having made a clear choice as to whether or not they had an interest in taking the necessary steps to become the best candidate.

Compensate Positions Based on Their Relative Worth to the Company

Businesses sometimes focus on maximizing the ownership position and compensation of family members, regardless of their ability to add value. This type of approach, where the sole criteria for engagement is family member status, is not appropriate in market driven companies.

If a business requires specialized expertise that is not currently held by family members, an attractive employment opportunity, including a competitive compensation package, should be provided to external candidates. Some in the family might consider this approach to be little more than diverting funds away from themselves; however, this view misses the real opportunity. When a company is able to attract a highly skilled candidate, at an appropriate level of compensation, it represents an investment being made in terms of corporate growth, marketplace competitiveness, and building future wealth for the family. The business must have the necessary infrastructure and skilled professionals to enable it to operate more independently of the founder and family, which is an important factor in the transitioning from one stage of growth and development to another.

Well-qualified candidates not only represent an opportunity for enhanced growth, through high achievement and strong job performance, they could also transfer skills and knowledge to others. Even in the case where a business leader has specific technical skills, such as Sydney and Sally, a younger professional could bring new and contemporary approaches to the company, which could be beneficial to all. These individuals also represent a future succession opportunity, in the absence of qualified family members who could take over the company.

In most cases, compensation should include a base salary and performance component (i.e., bonus, profit sharing, etc.), as well as an employee benefits plan (i.e., health, dental, insurance, etc.) and sales positions typically have an opportunity to earn a meaningful commission, based on results. It is important to keep senior members of a company focused on both short and long term results, which could be achieved through well structured incentive programs. Business leaders should also spend time developing their organizational chart in a manner that supports the company's strategic plan and objectives before seeking additional resources.

Once the role is understood, in the context of the company, business leaders should seek out information in terms of the appropriate compensation level as a starting point for developing an employment package. This information is often readily available, by way of industry salary surveys or interaction with a human resources professional. A salary range should then be developed for the position, providing opportunity for advancement and flexibility to adjust compensation based on a candidate's qualifications.

Performance-based compensation, such as bonuses and profit sharing, is an important component for attracting high quality candidates. Achievement-oriented individuals typically enjoy having performance targets and the opportunity to be compensated for generating results. This is a good approach for the company as well, since this type of compensation is only paid if and when the predetermined performance targets are met or exceeded. In addition, the level of results achieved could separate great performers from anything less, allowing any "mis-hire" situations to be quickly resolved.

Although the structure of performance targets could take various forms, a good approach is to combine those that pertain to the particular position (i.e., job tasks, professional development requirements, relationships with co-workers, etc.) with those that relate to the company (i.e., sales, profitability, successful launch of new products and services, etc.). This blended approach reduces the likelihood of efforts being focused in a manner that is solely in the best interest of an individual, perhaps at the expense of the business, as well as requiring teamwork to generate success.

Determine if Ownership is an Issue

In many family businesses, there is a belief that ownership of the company should not include external parties. In some Lifestyle Businesses or an extremely successful Market Driven Business that is comprised of several well-qualified family members, this might be appropriate; however, there are many entities whose performance and circumstances fall between these two extremes. These companies should consider the implications of making ownership opportunities available to those from outside of the family.

Ownership could be structured in a variety of ways, including an opportunity to acquire various share classes within the company (i.e., voting and non-voting, for example), stock options, phantom stock options (i.e., where no shares are issued, but compensation is based on the performance of the company's stock), and agreements to transfer shares at some future point in time. Given that structuring and implementing transactions and programs of this nature involves considerable effort, thought, and advisory fees for development and maintenance of the arrangement, ownership programs should not be pursued unless they are meaningful to the recipient. It is well worth the effort for the business leader to determine the degree of meaningfulness of this type of structure through discussion with potential candidates, as opposed to assuming the level of relevance, as an incorrect assumption could be a costly mistake either way. At the same time, it is important to ensure that the candidate would be a good fit for both their role and the company before entering into an ownership arrangement.

For key employees who are not family members, especially at a senior level and where a succession opportunity might exist, ownership could create both significant motivation for the employee and wealth generation for the company and family. Although the structure and specific requirements could vary, if a business leader is serious about growing the company to a new level, the issue of ownership is something that is certainly worth exploring, with the potential to provide more benefits than the "cost" of what is provided. Remember, the goal is to motivate and retain qualified non-family members, and this approach could be the difference between doing so and having them walk out the door, perhaps, to join your competitor.

Avoid Creating Employee "Classes" in the Company

Some businesses operate in a manner that suggests that there are special, albeit, unwritten rules for family members who are actively involved, as compared to non-family members. This type of "class" structure, where the sole defining factor is whether or not an individual is a family member, could be destructive for a company, particularly one that seeks to operate at a market driven level. Companies that fall into this category show their lack of development by way of these unsophisticated and detrimental practices.

Qualified non-family members, particularly those who hold key positions in the business, will not be enamored with scenarios where there is not a level playing field, in terms of what good performance could accomplish. Situations where compensation for external parties is determined based on the value of the job, while family members who are actively involved are compensated arbitrarily, and perhaps, at a premium, are likely to have the effect of driving out the former. This result puts the company back at Square One, if not further behind.

Family members should be compensated fairly, based on the value of the job that they perform, with any ownership or family-related compensation components being addressed separately. This type of approach creates a level playing field for all staff members, in terms of compensation and the value that they are expected to bring to the company. The same approach could be taken for other related areas, such as performance feedback, opportunities for advancement, and decision marking input.

Although these might seem like small things, utilizing this approach could be the difference between non-family members feeling that they have a real opportunity to contribute to the company, being fairly compensated based on their performance, and having access to opportunities for advancement, as opposed to facing a brick wall with a "family members only" sign on it. The only way to achieve this level of parity is through the appropriate documentation, processes, and attitude: everyone needs to sign an employment contract, undergo job interviews and performance reviews, share in team rewards, and understand their role and that of others. These areas must be supported by standard human resources policies, legal agreements, and company-wide implementation and conistent adherence to the rules.

Encourage Professional Development and Integration

Professional development, training programs, and access to skill-enhancing opportunities are critical in fostering a learning environment. Networking with others in a particular profession or discipline could be of particular importance, especially in situations where a qualified non-family member is brought into a company to provide a specific type of expertise.

In this scenario, the business leader and other members of the organization do not have the expertise that is being hired (i.e., engineering, accounting, digital technologies, etc.). Qualified non-family members who join a business of this nature hold an important role, as they are providing specialized knowledge and expertise that is essential for taking the company to a new level. These professionals could feel isolated in a company where there is not access to anyone at a senior or peer level that could provide mentorship and support. If this isolation persists, they might leave to pursue opportunities where they could have daily access to others who share their expertise.

Encouraging regular professional development and interaction with a peer group or professional association outside of the company could provide the necessary exposure to the resources that well-qualified non-family members require in order to feel connected to their profession. Many of the fees for these programs are tax deductible for the company and bring greater benefit than their cost. This approach could keep qualified non-family staff members motivated and performing well, transferring new knowledge to the business and minimizing the likelihood that these individuals would pursue relocation to a less isolating environment.

And for any business leaders who take the view that this type of professional development represents a risk to the company that their staff members might be recruited away by others, they need to remind themselves of what operating at a market driven level means. Great companies need talent, not staff members that nobody else wants.

Address Inappropriate Behavior

Despite a business leader's best intentions and communication efforts, some family members might still feel compelled to express their dissatisfaction with external parties holding key positions in the company. This unacceptable behavior does happen and must be addressed by the business leader immediately in order to avoid damage to the company, as well as the possible loss of qualified individuals

Family members must be reminded that the best interest of the business is the priority, and anything less than that comes at the expense of the company and the family as a whole. At the same time, non-family members must make a commitment to respectfully contribute to the growth of the enterprise as a whole, and that includes all staff members within it.

The steps that should be taken to correct inappropriate behavior could vary with the situation; however, whatever the approach, it must be effective in resolving the matter. If a business leader is at a loss as to how to address the problem, consulting a human resources professional could be helpful to achieve resolution. Failing to act is not an option, and everyone involved is seeking resolution, whether they realize it or not.

SUMMARY: DEFUSING THE FAMILY BUSINESS TIME BOMB

Minefields

- Business leaders that feel threatened by talented non-family members need an attitude adjustment. These individuals have the potential to add significant value to your company, so create an environment where they are motivated to perform at their best and celebrate their accomplishments!

- Do not underestimate the importance of the areas that are discussed in this chapter to non-family members; they matter tremendously and are necessary for long term engagement.

Tools

- Reconfirm your commitment to operate as a Market Driven Business and make the best decisions possible, in terms of seeking the most appropriate person to hold key positions, family member or otherwise.

- Being "the smartest person in the business" could be extremely lonely and not sustainable for professionals who seek daily interaction with others in their profession. Encouraging professional development and interaction outside of the company could be an important strategy in retaining qualified non-family members with specialized skills, in situations where the business leader(s) possess limited expertise.

- Recognize the value that a qualified non-family member could bring, including new and specialized knowledge, technical skills, a personal network, professionalism, and a high degree of motivation. These individuals represent an opportunity to energize your company, encourage others to perform better, and integrate new skills and expertise.

- Develop standard systems, policies, and procedures as the framework for operating effectively in a competitive market environment. Do not allow internal obstacles to detract from being of service to current and potential customers.

YOUR MISSION: Engaging Non-Family Members. How to Ensure that Valuable Resources Stay, Instead of Get Away.

`READY` **THINGS YOU NEED TO KNOW**

- Qualified non-family members represent a powerful opportunity to improve a company's performance and transfer useful skills and expertise, particularly in terms of businesses that do not possess a lot of professional or technical knowledge.

- Qualified external parties could represent a succession opportunity, in the absence of family members who do not have the skills or interest to do so. These situations should be compensated and treated in a manner that preserves this option.

- Qualified non-family members that consider joining a family business, for the most part, want to be treated fairly, in terms of compensation, input, and advancement opportunity. Failing to do so could result in these talented individuals leaving to pursue other opportunities, perhaps with competitors.

`SET` **QUESTIONS YOU NEED TO ASK**

- Does the company require expertise and/or additional help that cannot be provided by family members?

- In the case of qualified non-family members that are currently working in the company, are they being treated fairly, in terms of compensation, input, and opportunities for advancement?

- Does your company have employee "classes", in terms of family and external staff members?

- Does your company encourage professional development and peer interaction, particularly for those who hold professional designations and/or key positions?

- Are family members that are active in the company treating externally recruited staff members appropriately, and vice versa, or are there behavioral issues that require immediate resolution?

- Have any qualified non-family members left the company? If so, why?

- Have any qualified family members left the company? If so, why?

- Does your company have an appropriate succession plan, or should you be considering the potential for qualified non-family members to fulfill this role?

THINGS YOU NEED TO DO

- Identify any gap areas and action items to bring resolution, as part of the transformation planning process.

- Identify areas of the company where specific assistance and/or expertise is required. Set priorities in terms of which position(s) should be filled first and incorporate this into the annual operating and business plans.

- Obtain competitive compensation information for similar positions, by way of salary surveys or assistance from a human resources professional.

- Review your company's compensation structure, input and advancement opportunities, and other areas to ensure that inequity does not exist between family and non-family members. Resolve any differences to eliminate the potential for an employee class structure.

- Consider the opportunity for staging positions, where junior or inexperienced family members are not ready to hold a position. A qualified non-family member could hold the role for a period of time, transfer knowledge to the company, and act as a mentor to transition a family member into the job at some future point in time.

- Consider the status of your succession plan and determine if qualified non-family members are required to develop a suitable strategy.

DEFUSE DECISIONS YOU NEED TO MAKE

- Determine how the company's skill and workload needs would be handled, now and in the future. Are there qualified family members available or is looking to external resources a better solution?

- If you are ready to embark on the process of seeking a qualified non-family member, determine and implement the appropriate strategy for doing so.

✔ **Mission Accomplished:** When you look around your company and see individuals for the job they do, the value they bring, and the promise they hold, as opposed to seeing family and non-family members, you have established an environment without employee classes, where everyone is in a position to work as a team to their full potential. Recognize the power of this situation for what it is.

Planning for Crisis Situations
How to Survive Illness, Conflicts, Breakups, and Family Strife

Business owners Jess and Jonathan were 15 holes into their weekly golf game. Jess (aged 49) and Jonathan (aged 52) chatted about their developments over the past week as they made their way through the course on a hot and sunny summer day. This is the life!

Jess moved the discussion to a more serious note, speaking of a friend whose son had taken over the family business a couple of years ago so that his father, who was recovering from a hip replacement operation, could be less involved in the company. The arrangement seemed to work well for several months, but when market conditions changed, the company lost a few key customers, resulting in a drop in working capital. Unfortunately, the son lacked the knowledge and experience to address the matter and could barely meet payroll, resulting in his father having to return to the company, in the hopes of salvaging what had become desperate circumstances.

"Could you imagine facing that type of situation after leaving your company?" Jess asked Jonathan. "So much for retirement, not to mention the financial worries!". It was rumored that the father had helped his son acquire the company by accepting payment for his shares over several years, and with the company in trouble it was hard to assess the impact of doing so.

Jonathan told Jess about friends of his, Julie and Doug, who were going through a long and bitter divorce. Julie had replaced her father in managing her family's manufacturing business and her husband had taken on the role of Production Manager. With divorce proceedings in progress, Doug was of the opinion that he should be compensated for a portion of the company's significant growth, much to the dismay of Julie and her family. Jonathan commented that, with all the emotional angst, concerns about the company's financial future seemed like a burden that could have somehow been avoided.

The two friends moved to the 16th hole. It was mid-afternoon and the sun was very hot. Jonathan took off his hat, wiped his forehead, and stepped up to the tee box. He suddenly felt tense and exhausted by the heat. As he fell to the ground and gasped for breath, Jonathan looked up at the clear summer sky and wondered, "What is happening to me?"

THE ISSUES

Luckily for Jonathan, he was just dehydrated and recovered after drinking lots of fluids and resting; but, what if the reason for his collapse had been more serious?

Jess and Jonathan were right to be concerned about the scenarios they discussed. Crises such as these not only pose a risk to business leaders and their families, but could also put the company in peril, perhaps to a point where it cannot be salvaged. Since these situations impact both individuals and the company at hand, they compound the stress and loss felt by family members, as well as their economic well-being at a time when they are at their most vulnerable. Planning ahead is not only helpful, it is a must for protecting everyone involved, including the company, its staff members, customers, and of course, the family. Consider the impact of these typical crisis situations:

- **Illness.** As business leaders age, it is not uncommon for illnesses to arise, sometimes of a serious nature. An illness could force a business leader out of the company for a period of time or permanently and if there is no one available who could competently fill this role, the damage could be significant, if not disastrous. Companies that are dependent on the business leader are particularly at risk, such as in the case of many Lifestyle Businesses.

- **Death.** The death of a business leader, particularly when it is sudden or unexpected, is not only devastating, it also puts the future of the company and the family's economic well-being in peril. In the absence of a clear succession plan, family members often struggle to determine the best approach to go forward and might be forced to make important decisions at a time when they are at their weakest. This type of scenario could represent a double loss for the family: a beloved relative and the company's strength, direction, security, and financial performance.

- **Divorce.** The end of marital and common-law relationships among family members is painful on a personal level and could represent an even greater risk to the business. In the absence of proper planning and written agreements, individuals outside of the family (such as Doug) could hold the opinion that they are entitled to earnings or an ownership position in the company, which might (or might not) be reasonable. Either way, the uncertainty and lengthy time period that is often required to resolve such matters represent risks for both the family and company.

It is also important to remember that not only business leaders could be impacted by this situation, as it could apply to family members who might be less involved in the company (i.e., children, siblings, etc.). The risk is that the company could be held captive during the course of the disagreement, while its performance declines along with family relationships.

- **Conflict.** Family businesses are no stranger to the ups and downs of personal relationships, and this is particularly true for those that have not evolved to the professional management approach that is indicative of market driven status. Companies in this situation tend to function poorly and lose focus of what is important, due to the distraction that family conflicts and power struggles create. Instead of customers and market needs being the primary focus, staff members instead put their efforts into internal matters and divisive alliances, creating uncertainty in terms of how key roles and responsibilities should be fulfilled, among other things. This type of situation could be a very slippery slope, where companies descend into a routine of disfunction, something that might take years to unwind. It is important to recognize that these enterprises **are not** the choice of customers, strategic partners, or talented staff members.

  To this point, it can be very difficult for non-family members to deal with the uncertainty, lack of direction, and emotional conflict that is associated with these situations and many will simply leave for a more stable environment. Think about what this means: the skills, expertise, and experience that these staff members bring to a company are lost, thereby limiting the business' ability to grow, develop, and build value, to the benefit of the family. If family members *must* have something to argue about, it should be how they let this happen!

- **Insufficient Succession Planning.** When business leaders fail to effectively develop and implement a succession plan, this mistake could escalate soon after transition occurs, creating a crisis situation for the company. Recall the concept of "imaginary succession", where a business leader does a superficial job of developing a transition plan, fails to consistently enforce expectations of what is required for family members to take over the company, or does not engage a qualified business advisor to keep the process on track. While a succession transaction might occur, it is unlikely that the successor has the necessary skills, resources, or ability to take the company forward, which could lead to a disastrous outcome (as with the son in Jess' story). The former business leader might have to step in to try to restore order, and if successful, be rewarded by having to develop a new succession plan (this time, one that works).

What is particularly problematic about this situation is the passage of time. A proper succession plan is typically years in the making, with the necessity to cover areas such as successor selection, training, experience, financing, and transitioning of relationships. Having to address the process again could require a developmental period of several years, at a point where the business leader might not have the enthusiasm or ability to do so.

- **Weak Business Leader.** In some situations, a company might grow or evolve to the point where the founder no longer has the ability or desire to keep up with the increasing requirements of their role. This might occur in situations where a company is of a technical nature, where dramatic changes have occurred in the industry and marketplace. In many ways, the new economy has put a lot of companies in this situation, and if a business leader does not, or is not willing to, recognize the gap between their skillset and what is required to successfully lead the company, its market position is at risk.

  In the past, the real damage has been done when this scenario was allowed to continue for a prolonged period of time, however, today's new economy of change and disruption sets the stage for a much more rapid rate of decline. Once this has occurred, it is difficult to be in a position to build value or successfully transition the company to someone else.

These scenarios represent common business challenges; however, the list is not exhaustive. Companies might find themselves in situations that they could not have expected, which is why sound planning and risk management strategies are so important.

The Bottom Line: The loss of a business leader, for a period of time or permanently, could be devastating to the company, especially in the case of a Lifestyle Business, where there might not be adequately qualified and experienced staff members to assume the role. In order to avoid the risks associated with this type of situation, it is critical to migrate to the professional management approach that is exemplified by a Market Driven Business.

THE SOLUTIONS

There are various areas to consider when addressing people-related crisis situations and their potential impact. The overriding objective should be to plan accordingly so that a company is safeguarded from these situations as much as possible, thereby enabling it to continue to operate without significant interruption or harm. In addition, it is important to establish an environment of professional management, one that enhances the capability of staff members, rather than facing harm from conflicts and similar problems. Let's consider some of the things that a business leader should do in this regard.

Operate as a Market Driven Business

This statement embodies the "so obvious, it's simple" mentality, where a business leader should seek to position their company in a manner that not only allows it to perform well, but also safeguards it from potential risks and harm. In reality, it typically takes several years and an ongoing commitment for a company to evolve to the level of a Market Driven Business and many never reach this level of development. Doing so represents an *investment*; however, it is one that a business leader will never regret.

At its core, this approach incorporates the concept of professional management, whether it is provided by family or non-family members, supported by appropriate systems, policies, procedures, and resources. This professional management framework is an important requirement to successfully build a company, as it provides the necessary depth and capacity for growth, as well as the ability to manage through challenging times. Although companies are often launched with enthusiasm and in times of market need, business leaders do not always recognize that the path ahead tends to be more challenging than not.

Companies that embody a professional management approach have the ability to spread responsibilities across various individuals, which helps to mitigate the risk that arises when a staff member is lost. Market Driven Businesses typically have the necessary depth and skills to continue operating during crisis situations or market volatility and adopting this type of approach is important for its safeguarding, as well as reducing its dependency on the leader.

Market Driven Businesses that are particularly strong also have senior leadership that is experienced in a range of situations, including changing economic and market conditions, technological advancement, competitive threats, and transactions, such as financings, mergers, or acquisitions. These experienced staff members recognize that the business environment is always changing, as well as the importance of understanding external trends, developments, and potential risks. This skillset is very important for managing in the new economy, as change is a constant that has never been more rapid and fluid than it is now.

Document Company Policies and Procedures

Founders could spend years developing their knowledge in a range of areas, including product/service design, business development, and their personal network, but not take a moment to safeguard this critical information. In an era when a company's knowledge base and intellectual property could walk out the door in text messages, emails, and other networking activities, it is more important than ever to document policies and procedures in a central location, including safeguards over how this information could be used.

This is particularly important, in terms of ensuring that the core knowledge and processes for managing the company are not simply "in the head" of the business leader, representing a significant risk in the event of their absence. Formal documentation also represents value to a successor or potential acquirer, as it means that they would not have to "start from zero" in developing this information, raising the likelihood that they would be in a position to operate successfully in the days after transition. This also mitigates the risk of a failed succession event, ensuring that a company has a documented foundation that is an operational guide, as well as part of it for the long term.

Use of employment agreements is an important mechanism for safeguarding corporate knowledge and intellectual property, by way of confidentiality, policy compliance, and code of conduct requirements. In the age of virtual information, where documents and intellectual property could easily be circulated with little thought to the consequences, this approach is critical for clarifying expectations and implementing safeguards. Some business leaders might shrug off these areas as "nice to have", but the sinking feeling that comes with the realization that a former, trusted employee has left with corporate knowledge that does not belong to them could result in a much different perspective, albeit too late.

Have a Formal Succession Plan

A succession plan is not only useful in times of selling a company, it is also of critical importance for implementation in crisis situations. This scenario is one that business leaders do not always consider, being of the view that they have lots of time to develop a formal succession plan. In reality, a business leader should start planning for their absence as soon as their take over a company, to ensure for its ongoing operation in any circumstance.

A succession plan not only ensures that timely and appropriate steps are taken to continue operations in the absence of the business leader, it also makes their wishes known so that family members do not have to struggle with determining the appropriate course of action. In situations where family members are not actively involved in the business, it could be difficult for them to navigate forward due to a lack of critical knowledge. Even in situations where family members are actively involved, a tragic or emotional loss could make turning their attention to the company difficult, increasing the risk of problems occurring in the short term, while next steps are being determined.

In the event of illness, death, or any other situation that gives rise to a business leader's absence for a prolonged or permanent period of time, a succession plan provides direction in a number of key areas, including:

- How implementation of the plan should occur and who is responsible for monitoring the process
- Who would assume the role of business leader
- How any vacancies of those who took over the business leader role(s) should be addressed
- How ownership positions should be adjusted (i.e., in the case of death or disability, the business leader's shares might be transferred to others or a family trust, etc.)
- Shifting or redistribution of responsibilities between various positions
- Training and professional development requirements
- Legal requirements, in terms of a transfer of ownership, signing authorities, appointment and resignation of offices, etc.
- Role of any key advisors, such as business, legal, accounting, tax, and insurance

- How relationships with financial partners, such as lenders, investors, and shareholders, should be managed

- Steps to take regarding transfer or sale of the company

Depending on the situation, a succession plan might make reference to the business leader's will. It is important to recognize that the purpose of a will is to address matters relating to the decedent's estate, and although it might be related to succession matters, the company must clearly "own" the plan in this regard so that its future is sufficiently addressed. To this end, the company must be treated as a distinct and separate entity in order to ensure that its operations do not get bogged down in processes that relate to the estate.

Put another way, although the personality of the company might be an extension of the business leader, it is a separate entity from a legal and tax perspective. Companies often have more than one shareholder or partner with legal rights under a shareholders' or partnership agreement, raising the importance of the business being sufficiently structured to stand on its own, in terms of its management, decision making, and succession, to name a few.

Have Proper Legal Documentation and Agreements

Many business owners tend to think that they do not need legal advice, unless a problem occurs. This attitude fails to recognize that the absence of competent legal advice and documentation could be putting the business and the family's financial future at risk.

Areas such as shareholders' agreements, proper share issuance and documentation, employment agreements, articles of incorporation, bylaws, and shareholder resolutions are just some areas where companies should seek qualified legal advice. Financings and business transactions, such as mergers, acquisitions, strategic partnerships, and sale of the company are specialized areas where it is not wise to "go it alone". The result of poor or no advice could be much costlier than the price of getting professional guidance, and this is particularly true in the case of the current environment, with new challenges and complexities arriving on a regular basis.

Business leaders should consult with their legal advisor to understand the implications and risks that might arise from the breakdown of marital or common-law relationships, in the case of themselves and other family members that are shareholders in the company. If appropriate steps are not taken, the business might be exposed to unnecessary risk, in terms of non-family members having reasonable claims against the company, which could lead to additional costs and strife within the entity and the family. Use of pre-nuptial agreements, for example, provides the opportunity to safeguard the business from this type of situation, and the best time to negotiate is typically in the early days, when ground rules are being established and relationships are amicable. This is true for both personal and corporate agreements.

Another important area to address is what is often referred to as key person insurance, where the company obtains life, disability, critical illness, or similar types of insurance for the business leader or other key positions. In this situation, the company is named as the beneficiary of the policy and, in the event of death or disability, insurance proceeds are paid to the business. This type of coverage could provide resources for implementing the succession process, engaging interim professional management, or settling the business leader's ownership position with the estate. A qualified insurance professional could provide possible structures and coverage arrangements for consideration that could be utilized in this regard.

Companies should also ensure that intellectual property is sufficiently protected, such as in the case of patents, trademarks, trade secrets, and copyrights. The level of importance associated with this area could vary with the nature of the business, however, those that have unique technologies, designs, or content that should be protected could represent future earning potential, regardless of who is leading the company. Lawyers who specialize in this area are in the best position to provide guidance and strategies to protect these important assets.

Recognize that the Best Interest of the Company Must Prevail

Most people could probably recall a family business, whether it is one that they know well or have heard about from a friend, where conflict amongst relatives is a typical occurrence. Whether it is a case of squabbling siblings, children who do not agree with how a parent manages the company, or spouses who do not see eye-to-eye, battles of this nature take their toll on a business. It does not matter if conflict is a daily occurrence or whether it is less frequent; the reality is that, in time, it could be emotionally draining, create alliances that pit people against one another, or cause some to withdraw from the situation completely. This is not a healthy or sustainable environment for anyone, be it the family, staff members, or the company.

The approach that is ultimately in best interest of the business is not negotiable, otherwise, the family is putting their own financial future at risk, as well as that of other relatives. Family businesses could be viewed as a double-edged sword: they benefit from the camaraderie and teamwork of a family, but are also vulnerable to the impact of close relationships that are often characterized by an abundance of emotions and personal history. When functioning well, a family unit could be unstoppable; conversely, the latent power of the family business time bomb, ticking loudly and ready to blow.

The solutions to successfully manage through these situations could vary, but the following key points are helpful in guiding family business leaders in times of conflict and a lack of harmony:

- **Re-enforce the Market Driven Business Approach.** It is amazing what a bit of perspective can do, which could be achieved by focusing family members and the company *outward*, in terms of what is required to successfully compete in the marketplace. This removes the emphasis from internal matters, including the basis of family conflict, which might (or might not) be relevant to the marketplace. Qualified non-family members, especially those at a senior level, could also provide a much-needed "reality check" in situations where family members are not focusing on what is important, such as why the company exists in the first place: meeting customer needs.

  Companies that get caught up in internal drama are essentially out of balance and need to be reminded that business leaders and staff members should be focusing *at least half of their time* on the marketplace (some positions will have an even larger portion of their time dedicated to doing so). This includes industry and market trends, competitive developments, customer needs, business development opportunities, networking, and external requirements, such as in the case of financial partners, legal, and regulatory areas. When this perspective is taken, it puts an entirely different focus on what is important and where time and effort should be invested.

- **Fix bad situations.** This might sound obvious, but it is not uncommon for conflicts and poor performance to continue within a family business for a prolonged period of time, with the business leader simply avoiding or ignoring the problem and hoping that the situation will change. This is not likely; in fact, the opposite is true in most cases.

As previously mentioned, staff members, especially those who are not part of the family unit, are looking to the business leader to resolve problems. Situations of conflict and poor performance not only damage the company's ability to function effectively, they also reduce the level of motivation of those who are performing well, leading to a bad environment that expands as each day passes, as well as unexpected departures.

Resolving a problematic situation with a family member could include termination of employment, share buyout, or other approaches. Some situations could be resolved by the parties agreeing to divide the company into separate entities or providing the opportunity for a family member to manage a separate division or related company. This approach might provide sufficient separation to eliminate day-to-day conflict, without sacrificing the company, its reputation, and position in the marketplace in the process. This approach should not be used, however, in situations of unacceptable behavior or performance, where the offender deserves nothing less than removal from the company.

Business leaders need to recognize that there is life after parting ways with situations that are not working. Moving forward with an alternate structure or fewer relatives in the company is not necessarily a bad thing; it might simply be what is necessary to allow the business to be successful in changing times, and perhaps, represents something that should have been done long ago.

Separate the Life Cycle of the Company from that of the Business Leader

In a lot of ways, this is what professional management and succession planning seek to do—create depth and reduce the level of dependence on the business leader, thereby protecting the company and allowing it to move forward.

Some family businesses really are their leader, as in the case of many Lifestyle Businesses, or the example of Vicky in Chapter 3. The problem with this approach is that growth is constrained by what the business leader alone can do, skills are limited, and the company is at risk, should the founder be lost. This situation is a risk to the family's financial future and puts a clear limit on what could be achieved by the company, despite all of the time and effort that the business leader has invested.

Viewing the business leader as an integral part of the company, but also taking the steps to create a separate life cycle for its operations and growth, provides clarity in terms of what is needed to become and stay successful. This includes professional management, incorporating skills and experience that the business leader does not possess, and other critical components to successfully compete in the marketplace. Take a moment to think about the power of this concept; one that essentially puts a company on the path of successful existence well beyond that of its founder, the next business leader, and future successors.

Having said that, achieving this level of separation requires a significant amount of work and is truly an investment in a company's ongoing performance, safeguarding, and transition value. A qualified business advisor could be helpful in establishing the necessary framework to separate the life cycle of the business leader from that of the company, as well as a valuable resource to keep the process on track.

When Disaster Happens, Get Help

If a family business is operating as a Market Driven Business and/or has a sound succession plan, it is in a far better position to face crisis situations; however, it will still encounter challenges. Crisis situations are never easy, and in the case of a company that is inadequately prepared or has experienced an unsuccessful leadership transition, the business might have significantly deteriorated.

A qualified business advisor could objectively assist in getting the company back on track, bringing experience and perspective to wade through the emotional aspects of the situation. Since they are not a family member, business advisors are well equipped to look at the situation for what it is, as opposed to dwelling on past grievances or taking sides. They might not be able to fix every problem or salvage every company, but are likely the best resource to provide an objective assessment and guidance.

Corrective action might include steps such as terminating staff members who are not fulfilling their role, suggesting interim professional management to hold key positions, revising a failed succession plan, or even selling part or all of the company. These solutions might not be ideal, but should, at a minimum, focus on salvaging the company's value, where possible, for the sake of the family.

If this sounds discouraging, it is probably due to the realization that there are many things that a business leader could have done in order to avoid arriving at this situation. Business leaders have *choices*, and the decisions that they make in terms of building their companies are often reflected at key points in their lifecycle, including in times of transition or trouble.

SUMMARY: DEFUSING THE FAMILY BUSINESS TIME BOMB

Minefields

- Some business leaders have a need for the company to be dependent upon them. This is not in the best interest of the company and speaks more about the personal needs of the business leader than the needs of others, including the family. This trap is best avoided!

- Considering legal assistance to be an unnecessary cost that is of little value is a naïve approach. Sound legal advice, in terms of proper agreements, documentation, and decision making guidance could save a company from the financial ruin that might ensue in the absence of doing so.

Tools

- Documenting your wishes for the company in your absence, by way of a sound succession plan or other strategies, provides clarity and removes a considerable burden from family members.

- The best sign of a business leader's success is when a team that could competently take the company forward is in place, in times of planned succession or crisis. A needy business represents weakness and missed potential.

- The professional management approach of a Market Driven Business could provide an important safety net when family dynamics spiral out of control.

YOUR MISSION: Planning for Crisis Situations.
How to Survive Illness, Conflicts, Breakups, and Family Strife.

`READY` THINGS YOU NEED TO KNOW

- Ignoring conflict between family members in a company is a dangerous approach, as the situation will not magically "sort itself out". Crisis situations have the potential to derail a family business and permanently damage relationships in the process.

- Operating as a Market Driven Business and having a sound succession plan could greatly mitigate the impact of crisis situations.

- A well developed succession plan not only helps a company to continue to operate and move forward in a timely manner, it also communicates the wishes of the business leader, eliminating the need for family members to struggle with determining what might be the best course of action, at a time when they are experiencing heightened emotions or loss.

- Separating the life cycle of the business leader from that of the company could bring focus to what steps should be taken to achieve stability and longevity, creating an opportunity to build wealth over a longer period of time. The two life cycles need not be the same.

- Proper documentation, including policies, procedures, and legal agreements are required in order to protect the company from crisis situations, particularly in instances of relationship breakdowns.

- In the case of disaster, get help. A qualified business advisor could provide the necessary objectively help to get the company back on track, as well as a network of advisory relationships.

`SET` QUESTIONS YOU NEED TO ASK

- Does the company have a sound succession plan that could be implemented in times of crisis?

- Does the company have appropriate documentation and agreements that protect it from crisis situations, such as the breakdown of marital and common-law relationships?

- Does the company have adequate key person insurance coverage that could provide proceeds to cover or offset the costs of succession or interim management in a crisis situation?

- Are there family members within the company who are no longer qualified to perform their role, due to technical advancements or a lack of interest?

- Are there conflicts among family members within the company that need to be resolved?

- Are there conflicts about the business among family members who are not actively involved in the company that need to be resolved?

- Does the company have its own life cycle, or is it dependent upon the business leader?

THINGS YOU NEED TO DO

- Identify any gap areas and action items to bring resolution, as part of the transformation planning process.

- Review the company's key agreements and determine if enhancements or updates are required.

- Meet with your legal advisor to discuss update of agreements or additional risk areas that should be addressed.

- Review your succession plan to ensure that it addresses all areas that would require attention in a crisis situation.

- Meet with a qualified insurance professional to determine the company's insurance needs and options for addressing them.

- Address any existing family conflicts in the company and explore options for resolution, including termination, dividing the company, or agreement to permanently resolve the matter.

- If your company is currently in a crisis situation and/or not performing well, get professional help from a qualified business advisor.

DEFUSE DECISIONS YOU NEED TO MAKE

- If you do not have a sound succession plan in place, one must be developed, including deciding how the company would move forward in your absence. This involves identifying a successor(s) or indicating that the company is to be transferred or sold upon your departure.

- In the event of an existing family conflict, the best interest of the company must prevail, which includes resolving the matter. As the business leader, you must determine the best course of action, remembering that this need not be done without professional advisory assistance.

✔ **Mission Accomplished:** When you view the business as a separate entity, rather than an extension of yourself, the opportunity exists for the company to move forward in a manner that is in its own best interest, in perpetuity, and to the ultimate benefit of the family. 🌳

7

When the Business Leaves the Family
How to Transition, Let Go, and Move Forward

Andrea, age 52, owns a tree farm and commercial greenhouse that she started 25 years ago. The company began by supplying a few local garden centres and has grown to the point where it delivers product to a large network of stores across the region. Her parents helped her get started, as passive investors in the company, and often remark, with a smile, just how much things have changed since the business' early days.

Andrea has decided that she would like to spend another four or five years running the company and then move on to the next stage in her life. During this timeframe, she would like to see continued growth in the company, but is not enthused by the prospect of doing so by building its customer base through the normal course of business. Andrea does not have a clear succession plan, and although her niece and nephew (both in their 20's) have worked part time in the business for years and shown some interest in taking over the company, they also each have their own career plans. There is not currently anyone in the company who could assume the leadership role.

As a result, Andrea is considering the option of merging with another company of a similar size or selling to a national player. She is also aware of a few large companies that might have an interest in acquiring the business at some point, but is not sure how to investigate this type of transaction. Andrea would like to identify other options to grow the company, if any, as it would be helpful to understand what the future could hold. She would like to develop a plan over the next six months that considers possible growth and succession options, in relation to the objectives that she has established.

THE ISSUES

Andrea is facing, perhaps, the most challenging situation her business has encountered since its initial startup period. Achieving growth in a company is never easy, but business transactions, such as mergers, acquisitions, or taking on a partner with an existing customer base could represent both opportunities and complications. Andrea is taking the right approach, in terms of identifying and understanding all of her options, as well as planning in a manner that meets her transition objectives.

When it comes to business transactions, there are two main areas of consideration, both of which have implications for the business leader, the family unit, and the company.

The Technical Aspects of the Transaction

Since mergers, acquisitions, and the sale of a business are specialized and highly technical areas, most business leaders require advisory assistance in order to successfully undertake a transaction of this nature. Expertise could be required in a range of areas, including tax, valuation, due diligence, financing, business advisory, and corporate/securities law. An experienced advisor could bring knowledge that covers more than one of these areas, such as a lawyer handling the corporate/securities law requirements and some of the due diligence work. Valuation and tax advice could be obtained through accountants with specialized expertise, often by way of a firm that offers a range of professional services.

Depending on the company's geographic location, specialized financial advisors could be more difficult to find, such as in the case of those whose background is in the area of private equity, investment banking, or large transactions. These advisors bring specialized knowledge and helpful networks, but it is important to recognize that their role in business transactions typically differs from that of financial institutions, such as banks and credit unions.

Although there could be exceptions, banks tend to fill the role of a senior, and perhaps, secured lender and are generally more comfortable with established companies that have steady operations. Private equity investors, on the other hand, tend to be comfortable with companies that have experienced significant levels of growth and are investors that hold shares, as well as lenders. The main issue is to recognize that different financial partners have different mandates and areas of focus, which might not be consistent with the company at hand.

Unless they have had previous experience, business leaders could have difficulty finding a financial partner that fits with the type of transaction that they are seeking, which could result in frustration associated with delays in moving forward. Raising capital tends to require far more effort than anticipated, which is why advisory assistance, planning, and allocating a sufficient amount of time to the process are so important.

Business leaders have a significant level of interest in the "price" of a transaction, regarding how much a company would have to pay (in an acquisition) or the amount that would be received (in a sale); this is understandable. There is often not a simple answer in terms of price or how it could be structured, as typical options include a cash payment and/or a range of remuneration structures, such as shareholdings, earn-outs, directorships, and consulting agreements.

The final amount is typically based on a "range of value" associated with the company at hand, as determined by a qualified business valuator. A company's price is also impacted by the negotiations between the parties, based the amount that one party is willing to pay and the other party is willing to accept. It the absence of arriving at this sense of fairness and common ground, a transaction is unlikely to occur. It is also important to remember that a company's value does not last forever, as changes in financial performance, market conditions, and industry developments could all impact valuation. Changes of this nature could occur more quickly than business leaders might expect.

There are various approaches to estimating value, most of which are quite technical. Generally speaking, approaches could include benchmarks based on the nature of the business and/or its industry, public company values, past financings, or similar transactions. The highly technical nature of this area, as well as the need to apply judgment in terms of how valuation approaches and information should be utilized increases the importance of working with a qualified valuation advisor, such as a Chartered Business Valuator (CBV).

In the end, negotiated values could vary from the "technical" range of value determined by the valuation process, such as in the case where there is a strong desire to acquire a company (strategic value) or sell it (liquidation value). These circumstances could impact the transaction value in the end, however, they do not diminish the importance of obtaining credible valuation guidance.

All of these issues should be considered by the business leader and any other shareholders well in advance of a transaction, to avoid a lack of familiarity with these concepts, but also to put the company in a position to generate its best value when the time comes. When a business leader is well prepared, it sets the stage for realizing value, as well as having various options, in terms of transactions that could be pursued.

The Cultural Aspects of the Transaction

Once a family business undergoes a merger or takes on a significant partner, it might not be the entity that it once was. In the case of completing an acquisition, the company's culture might live on; however, when all or a substantial portion of the business is sold, its familial aspects might cease to exist. The impact on the culture of a company, when new parties come in or take over, is something that should be carefully considered by the business leader in advance of undertaking a transaction.

In the case of a sale, this is not a surprise, as the new ownership might choose to operate the company in a manner that differs from that of the former business leader, one that might not be consistent with their values, beliefs, and practices. In the case of a merger or new partner, the impact on the company's culture could be more problematic, given that the business leader (or members of the founding family) are typically still involved on a day-to-day basis.

Situations could arise where the two parties are in conflict, perhaps over significant issues that relate to how the company should be managed, who should hold key roles, growth strategies that should be taken, ethical considerations, and so on. This could result in the parties not being able to work together, damage the company, or, perhaps, a need to undertake a transaction to reverse the arrangement.

The Bottom Line: When a business leader is considering their company's future, in terms of growth-oriented transactions, succession to another party, or outright sale, both the technical and cultural aspects should be fully investigated, given the potential for substantial impact on the entity going forward. In order to begin, however, business leaders must ask themselves: Is my most compelling role to continue to lead the company, steward the family's wealth and values to the next generation, or realize value by transitioning to someone else?

The answer to this question could have a huge impact on both family dynamics and the business, to propel its presence in the marketplace from a commercial success to a position of leadership and lasting legacy. It is important to know how and when to do so, especially in the face of the new economy, where a variety of factors have come together to challenge the future and longevity of many enterprises.

THE SOLUTIONS

Before addressing options that business leaders could consider, in terms of succession and transactions, it is important to consider the landscape of the new economy, as it provides valuable context. Current trends and marketplace challenges have made it increasingly difficult for business owners to successfully transition their companies, in the absence of having developed a plan to do so over the long term. It is in the case of succession where the crux of the Family Business Time Bomb can be found. Consider these factors:

- **Increased levels of competition.** Many companies have delayed the succession process, which means that there are more businesses seeking their next leader. Demographics have an impact in this regard, as business leaders of the Baby Boom generation continue to age, with younger groups who could be the best target for ownership being relatively fewer in numbers and often lacking the financial resources to undertake a transfer of ownership.

- **A limited number of qualified successors.** Since the business leader role requires a particular blend of skills, experience, and interest, many in the target age group are not realistic candidates. Add to this the requirement of raising capital to support a transfer of ownership, in the event that the departing business leader is not willing (or able) to accept payment for their shares over a period of time, and the number of potential successors is further reduced.

There is an additional consideration for family businesses in this regard, as many members of the next generation who could be successors are no longer an option. This could be due to various reasons, such as having other interests, living in a different geographic region, or the nature of the family relationship at hand. One of the most prominent reasons, however, is a lack of opportunity to assume the leadership role, be it real or perceived.

This situation could occur for various reasons, such as business leaders not giving the impression that succession is an option, staying in the role too long, or inconsistent messaging.

As demographics include longer lifespans (which is something to celebrate), retirement has become less traditional, as people work longer. From a succession standpoint, this could create uncertainty for the next generation, as business leaders' express plans to "step back" or bring potential successors more into the workings of the company, only for years to pass with no tangible steps having occurred.

Understandably, the next generation must plan for their own future and although their previous expectations might have included taking over the family enterprise, the actions of their business leader relatives have made this a much less likely outcome. Instead, younger family members decide to pursue other opportunities, leaving behind the shock and dismay of those who realize that they have lost their succession plan (remember imaginary succession?).

- **Companies that lack marketplace relevance.** In situations where a business leader has not kept up with industry, market, and competitive developments, or in the case of an entity that has performed at a lifestyle level for a prolonged period of time, a company could find itself without a future. As discussed in previous chapters, these companies are not marketplace leaders and might require a significant amount of investment to be sustainable, both of which tend to result in being a better candidate for a windup than anything else.

Although opportunities could exist for new partners, mergers, acquisitions, or raising capital, the only companies that are likely to be successful are those that are in a *strong market position*. As a result of these circumstances, business leaders need to fully appreciate the competitive environment that they are facing, when it comes to succession. The new economy could be characterized as a buyer's market, making transition of a company to someone else much less of a given than it has been in the past. It is with this context in mind that succession and business transactions can now be considered.

Options for Transitioning a Business

A well-prepared succession plan is an integral part of any company's strategy and is of particular significance to family businesses; this should be second nature by now. Business leaders must consider and plan for their eventual exit, by giving thought to a range of potential growth-oriented transactions. This section addresses the typical types of transactions that business leaders encounter.

Taking on a Partner

As in Andrea's situation, one manner in which a business could grow is by taking on a partner with a customer base or "book of business" that would be brought to the company. This type of approach is more common in some industries, such as professional services (i.e., accountants, lawyers, etc.) or other types of service providers. Having said that, some product-based companies have strong customer relationships that could be transitioned to another entity.

In this scenario, one or more individuals might join the business, typically at a senior level, to create a larger customer and revenue base, thereby increasing the size of the company. There are certainly benefits to this type of approach, including relative ease of the transaction, staging growth without taking on too much change at once, and ability of the business leader to maintain control of the company, assuming that the new partner's customer base represents the smaller piece of the pie.

In this type of transaction, there is typically less of an impact on the culture of the company, as only one or a small number of individuals is being added to an existing and often larger entity. This means that new entrants are more likely to have to adapt to the existing culture, as opposed to bringing a new attitude and approach to doing things and imposing it on the company. There is also often an element of comfort, as both parties work and have experience in the same industry or line of business, and as a team, might be able to broaden their product or service offering, to the benefit of the company and its customers.

A partnership approach, however, is not without important areas that should be fully addressed before entering into a transaction, including the following:

- **Non-disclosure and non-competition agreements.** It could be frustrating to spend a considerable amount of time exploring a transaction with a potential partner, only to find that the arrangement is not workable. What is even worse is a failure to appropriately protect your company prior to entering into these conversations, such as through a non-disclosure agreement

(NDA). Doing so protects the company from the other party utilizing information that is shared, in the event that a transaction is not pursued. Keep in mind that many, if not the majority, of conversations of this nature **do not** lead to a transaction.

In addition, shareholder and partnership agreements should include clauses that address confidentiality, non-competition, and non-solicitation, among other areas, to govern the parties during the course of the arrangement, but also in the event that a decision is made to separate. Doing so establishes a foundation that protects a company from having its employees and customers approached by the other party, as well as requirements that govern competitive behavior.

Although many business leaders might expect that professionalism and integrity should be a given, there are unfortunately many situations where such standards are not upheld, resulting in costly losses, ambiguity, and broken relationships. As a result, it is critical that these areas be identified and addressed at the commencement of investigating any new relationship, so that there is clarity in terms of what the rules are. Working with experienced legal counsel is a necessary requirement to do this effectively.

- **Partner selection.** The key to successfully completing this type of strategy is to choose potential partners very carefully and undergo a thorough due diligence and vetting process to ensure that the business opportunity is substantiated and that compatibility exists, in terms of work style, character, and vision for the entity going forward. A qualified business advisor could be of valuable assistance in this regard, possessing the experience to conduct due diligence activities, as well as provide an objective viewpoint. This is very important, as many partnerships are not successful due to the parties failing to take a sufficient amount of time to assess their compatibility.

The trap of how this could occur is easy to identify: an immediate need for additional capacity, attempt to combat competitive pressures, lack of transaction experience, or the typical "rose-coloured glasses" that are associated with young relationships. The parties view one another as the match they have been seeking, focusing only on areas of commonality (real or imagined), without recognizing how different or incompatible they might be. This could lead to undertaking a transaction too quickly, and when success does not occur, the process of unwinding a relationship could be time consuming, expensive, and frustrating.

The interests and health of the company must always take precedence in the decision-making process. A qualified business advisor is in a good position to ask the right questions and remind participants of how success could best be realized, and it might just be a decision to not move forward with the transaction at hand.

- **Implementation planning.** Successful implementation does not just happen, nor do parties always have the same thoughts around how it should occur. Coming to an agreement in this regard could be challenging, and any partnership or collaborative opportunity requires a plan detailing how the transaction would occur and what changes are necessary to both the new partner's current way of operating, as well as that of the existing family business. This approach provides a clear path for implementation and addresses any areas of conflict before the transaction occurs, allowing the parties to determine if success could be achieved.

In practical terms, this could be addressed by way of various documents and processes, including the company's shareholders agreement, strategic plan, action planning and implementation, and other transactional terms. This requires both parties to dedicate a sufficient amount of time to determine how the arrangement would work, reducing the likelihood of misunderstandings and problem areas arising later. There should also be a clear plan that outlines the steps that would be taken in the event that things do not go as anticipated.

- **Leverage opportunities.** Partnership and merger opportunities are often attractive due to the potential to reduce expenses, by way of identifying areas of duplication and better utilizing capacity; this concept could be referred to as leverage. In order to build leverage, it is important to identify opportunities for new partners to fulfill their role by utilizing existing staff members and resources within the family business, as opposed to bringing their own cost structure.

The next step is to make leverage plans a reality, which could be more challenging than expected, in situations where the new partner retains their own systems and staff members, instead of integrating into the family business' existing infrastructure. It is not uncommon for companies that undergo this type of transaction to fail to take the necessary steps to *implement the strategy*, as it could be easier in the short term to avoid the effort and angst associated with making the necessary changes, leading to inefficiencies, conflict, and poor performance. Business advisors could be helpful in terms of identifying opportunities to generate leverage, as well as providing the specialized skills to make it happen.

Business leaders might sometimes hold that view that taking on a new partner is "no big deal" or "doesn't require a lot of work". As the above noted list indicates, this type of transaction does require a thorough amount of diligence and investigation, to ensure that outcomes are only of a positive nature.

Merging with Another Company

Merging a family business with another company has some similarities to the concept of a collaborative partnership; however, it typically represents a more significant level of change, as it might involve parties of a similar size and identifying the dominant culture, leader, and approach going forward could be up for negotiation. Two companies of similar size might see a number of benefits in coming together, such as a broader product and service offering, increased revenue and customer base, and more resources for achieving additional growth in the future.

There are various merger related situations that a family business could encounter, all of which cannot be addressed here. Consider the following possible situations, which represent both opportunities and risks to a family business:

- **An opportunity for short-term growth.** A merger transaction creates a larger company, and if managed properly, a more profitable business. Growth could occur more quickly than if the family business continued to operate on its own, through the normal course of acquiring additional customers, one at a time.

  Successful growth from a merger could set the stage for additional opportunities in the future, where the merged company might be large enough to attract the interest of a larger entity, resulting in an acquisition that could provide an exit for the family business leader. This staged approach requires planning, sound implementation, and a demonstrated track record of growth. Business advisors could be helpful in assisting in these areas, as well as bring a professional network to attract the next transaction.

- **An opportunity for succession.** A business leader might undertake a merger in the absence of a succession plan, as the company that merges with the family business could have better resources to take the combined entity forward at some future point in time. Put another way, where a family business lacks potential successors, a good strategy could be merging with a company that has more depth at a senior level.

- **Cultural risks.** As discussed in the previous section, selecting a party to join forces with should be done very carefully, and this is of heightened importance in a merger scenario, due to the size and strength of the parties typically being more equal. If a business leader does not select a party with a consistent approach and philosophy as to how the company should be operated, significant conflict and dispute could occur. Under a merger scenario, the business leader might no longer be able to control how the company operates, which could put at risk their desire to be involved going forward, as well as in the case of family members.

When a merged enterprise finds itself in this situation, the result could include the company performing poorly, breaking apart, or ultimately being sold to one of the parties (or someone else), all of which could be costly and emotionally draining. When this occurs, business leaders tend to be at a loss to understand how it all happened, having a new appreciation for the importance of the selection and due diligence of merger candidates, in terms of generating future success.

Mergers represent complex transactions and professional advice is required to provide guidance regarding the appropriate terms and conditions, due diligence, negotiation, and financing considerations. The importance of selecting the "right" company to merge with cannot be overstated, as the business could be fundamentally changed going forward.

Acquiring Another Company

A family business could achieve growth by acquiring another company to create a larger revenue, customer, and resource base going forward. The difference between a merger and an acquisition is that, in the case of an acquisition, the family business would retain its control over the existing company, as well as the acquired entity. In a merger transaction, control of the new company is typically shared in some manner. As a result, an acquisition typically renders cultural issues to be of lesser importance, as the approach of the acquiring company tends to remain largely intact going forward (the only exception to this might be in the case where the intent is for the acquired company to remain as a completely separate entity, one that is not integrated with its parent).

However, it is of significant importance to verify the substance of the opportunity, to confirm that the actual circumstances are consistent with what the business leader believes to be the case. This could be as straightforward as conducting thorough due diligence to confirm the strength of the products and services, financial position, market potential, and management team, areas where a qualified business advisor or lawyer with due diligence experience could be of assistance. A greater challenge, however, is being able to get a sense of the character of the company, in terms of the manner in which it operates and assessing if this represents an opportunity that is conducive to a successful acquisition. Although the acquirer ultimately determines the manner in which the acquired business would operate, it is much easier to do so if the transition occurs smoothly and the entities are well matched, in terms of compatibility.

An important component in doing so is to understand the role of existing staff members and their importance to the company, to develop a plan to integrate and maintain key resources going forward or eliminate positions that represent duplication or are not required. In the absence of a succession plan, the acquired entity might have resources that could succeed the family business leader at some point in the future, representing a benefit to the company. Regardless, the nature of the transaction at hand should help to provide guidance, in terms of what actions should be taken.

Professional advice is required to successfully complete an acquisition, in terms of fundamental areas such as valuation, tax, accounting, and legal assistance. In terms of the "business" aspect of the transaction, it could take a period of time for a new owner to fully understand what drives a company forward, what made it successful in the past, and what would keep it relevant to the marketplace in the future. New owners often fail to maximize this type of potential, due to a tendency to quickly fall back into their typical routine, perhaps lacking the ability to see "what could be". Professional advisors bring the necessary skills and perspective to develop business models and plans that capitalize on market opportunities and generate growth for what is essentially is a new enterprise.

Sale of the Company

A sale transaction represents the most significant change to a family business, as if an independent party is the purchaser, the company would no longer be of a "family" nature. This has important implications for both the business leader and family members.

Business Leader

In the event of a sale transaction, the business leader might no longer be a part of the company; this could be a planned and desired outcome or a difficult transition. In many cases, the business leader has spent a long period of time building the company and might have a strong attachment to it, as well as clear views as to how it should be managed. With a new owner, these views might not be appreciated, shared, or of any relevance, which could be the case in a situation where a business leader lacks the skills to take the company to its next stage of growth.

Opportunities might exist, however, for the family business leader to continue to be involved with the company after the sale transaction, by way of a contract or specified role where they could add value (i.e., technical areas, product development, customer relations, special projects, etc.). The new owner might benefit from having the family business leader remain with the company for a period of time to transition responsibilities, relationships, or provide advice in certain areas.

This type of arrangement has the potential for success, as the family business leader typically has areas of expertise that could be passed to new ownership, but challenges might also exist. It might be difficult for a family business leader to be part of a company that they no longer control and they might not agree with some of the decisions and approaches that are being taken. Since the family business leader is no longer in control, they typically would not have a decision making role, which could lead to frustration and conflict. Family business leaders should be careful when considering this type of arrangement and recognize that it might be difficult to fulfill.

There are some approaches for ongoing involvement that could be taken, however, and the level of compatibility of the parties would impact the potential for success. Options to consider include the following:

- **Short term contracts** of a year or less, to help transition the company to the new owner could be workable, provided that the role does not include a decision-making component, as this could be confusing and frustrating for everyone involved. The new owner must be in a clear position to take the company forward, without ambiguity or interference, perceived or otherwise, from the former business leader. Instead, the former business leader should act as a resource to help the new owner become familiar with the company.

- **Working on an ongoing contract basis** in specific project areas could be helpful to both the former business leader and the new owner. This approach would allow the former business leader to work on projects that might be of personal interest, perhaps utilizing their network to bring additional growth opportunities to the company. It might also allow the former owner to be compensated on a "success" basis, where the company would only pay if and when a deal is closed.

- **Advisory arrangements,** for a specified period of time, where the former business leader is available to provide advice to the new owner outside of day-to-day operations. This arrangement could take the form of providing knowledge, relationships, problem solving, or mentorship.

Should the family business leader wish to continue working in some capacity after the transaction, but not with the company, careful consideration should be given to the impact and negotiation of non- competition clauses that might be part of the deal. It is not uncommon for an acquirer to prohibit the business leader, and perhaps family members, from starting a similar new company or working with a competitor for a certain period of time after the sale transaction closes. Family business leaders should work closely with their advisors to understand the impact of this requirement and negotiate accordingly, particularly in instances where an income is requited after the transaction is complete.

Entrepreneurs rarely retire, as it is just not in their nature. Therefore, part of any sales transaction must include a clear and thoughtful glimpse into the "afterlife", to properly manage expectations and considerations going forward.

Family Members

In the case of family members who have a passive involvement in the company, a transaction might represent sale of their shares and a realization that the business is no longer a part of their lives; this could be a good thing, but could also change family dynamics. Conversely, the impact on family members who are actively involved in the company could be much more significant, as they might no longer have a job.

In the case of family members who continue to remain employed with the company after it is sold, they could be comfortable continuing under new ownership, but might be more likely to find it difficult to remain in this type of situation. They might not be comfortable with how the company is being managed, the direction that it is taking, or could simply miss the way that things used to be when the business was owned and managed by their family. This could result in family members choosing to leave the business and having to find alternate employment, which makes the terms and negotiation of non-competition clauses particularly important.

All family members will have to contemplate how they would replace the income that they were receiving from the company, either actively or passively, and this is something that should be fully considered prior to the sale of the business. Professional advisors could assist in structuring the sale transaction so that the proceeds could be received in a manner that is tax efficient for the recipients; however, the amount that is ultimately realized is dependent upon the value of the company and the negotiations between the parties.

In short, a new "life plan" is required—for the business owner, family members who worked in the company, and other passive investors and stakeholders, including employees, all of whom must address this personal and financial change. Doing so could be stressful, and the significant sums of money that are often involved reinforces the importance of thoughtful preparedness, skillful navigation, and advice.

It goes without saying that a sale transaction is complex, requiring various professional advisors to properly investigate, structure, and close. Receiving this type of qualified assistance could result in the effort that has been invested in the family business over many years being fully realized. Without it, many highly successful companies have met an early demise, to the detriment of the family, staff members, customers, and the community.

Moving Forward

Successful transition is a product of sound planning, strategy, and implementation. When business leaders take tangible steps to develop a strong performance track record, understand industry and market trends, and identify possible options for transition, they are in a good position to realize value when a transaction occurs. After years of spending the majority of their time and effort building their company, this achievement could represent financial success, but also the ability to close the chapter on their own terms. It is this freedom that could be particularly fulfilling.

Having said that, it is important to take the time to contemplate what the next stage of life might include, be it a merged company, larger business, or entity that has left the family. Change could create stress, even if it is from the relief of resolving a succession problem or family conflict that had been lingering for years. Business leaders should ensure that they tap into supportive resources, including advisors, friends, and family members. Most who have led companies know that the journey is never boring; may the outcome of transition be a path that leads to even better and more fulfilling days ahead!

SUMMARY: DEFUSING THE FAMILY BUSINESS TIME BOMB

Minefields

- Failing to recognize the impact of the new economy on your company could result in a business that has no other option than to windup. Understand the issues that impact your company and seek professional advice to ensure that the right strategies are in place.

- Underestimating the need to carefully consider continued involvement with a family business after a sale transaction can be problematic in the end. The company might undergo considerable change, making it impossible for family members to successfully integrate into the business.

- Failing to carefully consider income requirements for family members going forward can lead to unexpected circumstances. Non-compete clauses could be structured in such a manner that continued involvement in the marketplace for a period of time might not be permitted, which could lead to financial strain. This area must be carefully negotiated and understood.

Tools

- Carefully consider the impact of a business transaction on your company, particularly in terms of cultural fit and approach. Partners or merged companies that cannot work together could do irreparable damage to the business, its value, and be costly to unwind.

- Thoroughly investigate potential partner and merger candidates and take the time to get to know them. Patience is better than a quick decision.

- Decide whether potential partners are the right stewards of the company's future, without you in it. If you want the company to survive independently of your guidance and control, this is your primary responsibility as its leader.

- Always get qualified professional advice when undertaking a business transaction. Experienced advisors work much more efficiently and provide better advice than those with less knowledge and at a lower cost. At this important time, it is not wise to put your company at risk.

**YOUR MISSION: When the Business Leaves the Family.
How to transition, let go, and move forward.**

READY THINGS YOU NEED TO KNOW

- The new economy has resulted in a host of challenges that impact both succession and business transactions: rapid industry and marketplace change, technological disruption, global markets, and demographics. All of these could impact the sustainability and transition potential of a company.

- There are various growth strategies that a business could take, through the course of normal operations, taking on a partner, merging, or acquiring a company.

- Transactions represent opportunities for succession and could be particularly useful for a business leader who does not have a plan in this regard. Examples include increased resources through a partnership, merger, or acquisition, or the business leader selling their ownership position to a partner or shareholders of a merged company at some future point in time.

- Bringing new partners into the company or merging could have an impact on the culture of the family business. New entrants might have a management philosophy that is not consistent with that of the business leader, which could "upset the applecart", with both personal and financial implications.

- Business transactions are complex and require qualified professional advice in a number of areas in order to be successful.

SET QUESTIONS YOU NEED TO ASK

- How has the new economy impacted your company?

- What new economy risk factors are yet to be addressed?

- Has there been a change in your succession plan that requires consideration of other options?

- Are there individuals or parties that are worthy of consideration as potential partners or merger candidates?

- Are there companies that should be investigated for potential acquisition?

- Do you have professional advisory resources that could assist with conducting a business transaction?

- Are there reasons why the company should remain in the family or why it should be sold?

- In the event of a sale transaction, what are the income and ongoing employment requirements of family members?

THINGS YOU NEED TO DO

- Identify any gap areas and action items to bring resolution, as part of the transformation planning process.

- Review your business plan and recent financial performance to determine if growth targets are being met. If actual performance is below budgeted levels, consider the impact of other options for growth, including partner, merger, and acquisition models.

- Review the competitive landscape of your industry and assess the company's performance and position. If your business is either in danger of falling behind or has been displaced in the market, consider options for growth.

- Consider what "life after the business" looks like and plan accordingly.

DEFUSE DECISIONS YOU NEED TO MAKE

- Determine your level of interest in continuing to lead and grow the company. Identify the options for the company's future and select those that are worthy of investigation.

- Determine whether or not the business leaving the family is a realistic option.

- Consider how to select the right advisors to assist with the chosen path of transition, merger, acquisition, or sale.

✔ **Mission Accomplished:** Building a family business to a point where it has options for growth and succession, including by way of the normal course of operations, admitting partners, or making acquisitions provides strength in numbers for the company and the family. Choices, as opposed to forced options, are a good thing, and this requires advance planning, as the right successor could be just around the corner.

8

Managing the Risks We Know: Taxes Really Matter

Carol and Roger looked back at their family business ventures with fondness over their anniversary dinner. It had been an interesting couple of decades. They recalled how they came to take their future into their own hands: each of them, with two little children in tow, had lost their corporate jobs in the same year. It was a defining moment for their family unit: they wouldn't let that happen again. Instead, they would take control of their future and start their own independent business venture.

Carol and Roger were prepared to put their savings on the line and take on the risks of starting their own business. Often, they had to wait for their revenues to materialize and there was never a guarantee of a wage, vacation, sick leave, or overtime. But, the two of them were talented and resourceful and worked hard. Soon the revenues came, and with that, a new relationship with CRA—the Canada Revenue Agency.

It started with good news. As employees, CRA's share of their earnings was always deducted off the top—"first dollars out"—leaving a smaller amount for savings. But now, there were so many more deductions available to reduce taxable income. Corporate tax rates were much lower, too, leaving bigger dollars in the company to invest for growth. These "first dollars earned" were their own to leverage.

But the trade-off was an onerous burden of proof. Carol and Roger made it their business to comply with CRA's filing requirements. They understood the available tax planning opportunities and used them to their advantage, as was their right. But lately, even their professional advisors had difficulty receiving reliable interpretations of how many of the new tax laws applied to their business. This uncertainty brought with it the constant risk of an unexpected audit.

Yet, as their children grew to embrace the family firm's opportunities over the years, they all knew something valuable had been built: a company that boasted a solid base of satisfied clients, employed dozens of people in the community, and consistently delivered on business plans with precision. Now, the challenge was to stay ahead of marketplace disruptors and plan for succession, despite new tax rules, such as on the distribution of dividends!

As they cherished the last moments of what had been a lovely anniversary dinner, Carol and Roger could not know that another obstacle to their retirement plans would arrive tomorrow: a CRA audit letter.

THE ISSUES

It is estimated that there are close to three million[2] small businesses in Canada, which operate enterprises of every type. From professional practices, to farming and fishing, to independent consultants, writers, performers or tradespeople working in the service industry, they share a common thread: these self-employed people willingly invest their time and money—and passion—in the hopes of earning a living, and down the road, a return on their investment in their enterprises.

They often wait long periods of time before taking adequate earnings out of their company. No one is paying for their retirement, health care, vacation, overtime, or severance packages either. Business owners truly rely on themselves to provide for their livelihood, as well as that of their families, in many cases.

What often results is a "blend" of two lifecycles: that of the business and that of the owners. The extent to which the future goals for each are managed goes a long way to mitigating risks to two precious resources: time and money. Planning is necessary because the two lifecycles eventually take a separate path, as one will outlive the other. Will each remain healthy along the way? Who will the ultimate beneficiaries be? Will it be the owners, the family, the employees, the community? Or, will it be the CRA that walks away with the lion's share of accumulated wealth in the company? This unpredictable disruptor is a constant nemesis.

The ideal financial planning process works on a continuum, in a multi-stakeholder environment that anticipates financial peaks and valleys that both the business and the people who invest in it will inevitably experience. It is always focused on the end goal: *what matters is what you keep*; both in the company and in the pockets of the shareholders and employees who are engaged in the enterprise.

Like people, businesses also have lifecycles. Structured properly, with the right people, processes, and strategic plan in place, a successful company will continue to grow, regardless of whether the owners are present, through multiple business stages. Its lifecycle, in fact, can last several generations.

Human beings, on the other hand, have a limited lifeline. Their diminishing time is often spent in the long hours it requires to meet the future demands of a business—forever a dependant—instead of in care of their

2 Statistics Canada July 2018, The Entry into and Exit out of Self-employment and Business Ownership in Canada by **Douwere Grekou** and **Huju Liu for the period** 2001-2013

personal health and relationships. The relationship between the precious resources of time and money requires a careful balancing act.

Enter the nemesis: CRA. A special and reluctant relationship that business owners have, one that is high maintenance and demanding. It requires, by threat of large penalties, that business owners become unpaid tax collectors for the government. With little or no training or reliable information, they must make and remit mandatory statutory payroll deductions, collect various sales taxes on revenues earned, and remit periodic instalment payments in anticipation of net profits of the business, if any. CRA must be paid to the penny and on time, and the penalties for failing to do so are steep.

Expensive, meticulous recordkeeping is also subject to periodic audit with short response periods. This produces a constant risk that CRA will disallow the business owner's interpretation of extremely complex tax laws, for several years into the past, producing an unanticipated tax liability that must be paid immediately, or gather enormous interest charges. Add to this the fact that complex tax rules can change dramatically and on short term political whims. This can throw off even the most perfected balancing act.

The Bottom Line: Family businesses are left with this stark reality: throughout a personal lifetime of risk taking, unpaid labor, and the savvy skills that are necessary to out-maneuver marketplace obstacles that challenge the survival of the company, new and unexpected taxes—and a shifting burden of proof from one generation to the next—could quickly erode the significant human and financial capital that are required in order to fund the lifecycles of multiple stakeholders.

It is a ticking time bomb that could explode at any given time, one that requires constant monitoring, as well as immediate and specialized help.

THE SOLUTIONS

Business ownership is all about risk management. In securing an unpredictable financial future, determining what can be controlled is an important first step. Given that the CRA is such a large and unpredictable force, there are two basic strategies for keeping it at bay: first, invest in solid bookkeeping resources. Since your responsibilities with CRA can occur as often as every two weeks for payroll, and monthly for sales tax and instalment remittances: these areas need to be managed on a timely and reliable basis.

Second, it is critical to invest in strategic, integrated financial planning that anticipates taxes on both income and capital invested in the business and how to flow it through to the various individuals who are affected by investment in the company—in terms of salary, bonuses, dividends, or capital gains. Doing so provides the opportunity to best take advantage of the tax preferences available and leverage the time value of money.

Tax planning, in fact, provides an annual trigger for investment, retirement, succession, and estate planning; an opportunity that pays multiple returns on the investment of time and money. It makes sense to have tax specialists—in personal, corporate, cross-border, and trust taxation—on your team throughout the business lifecycle.

Clearly, the successful stewardship of income and equity generated by the family business requires a multi-stakeholder approach. Long term planning for the financial future of both the company and many people who are dependent upon it requires one common strategy in which everyone is aware and engaged. In fact, long term outcomes will always be compromised when a single solution is attempted or deferred to a later point in time.

But how do you find the specialists that are required in order to bring your financial team together? It is a common problem that many family business leaders face and find frustration in, to the determinant of their financial goals. This challenge ties back to realizing the simple, reasonable goal that many business leaders have: keeping more than CRA may take.

Finding a qualified bookkeeper. It is truly surprising how difficult this can be. There are many service providers in the marketplace who have the ability to enter data into a sophisticated bookkeeping software package. In fact, new technology exists today to bypass the human being who traditionally performs the data entry function, replaced by an end-to-end solution that snaps pictures of receipts, enters the numbers into the software, and flows it through to financial statements and CRA reporting structures. Likewise, income receipts are electronically deposited to financial institutions and flowed through bank accounts, financial statements, and various CRA reporting requirements.

Although technology can be a wonderful thing, in terms of increasing efficiencies and performing mundane tasks, it can provide a false sense of security, in that it lacks the "thinking" and oversight components that are required in order to get to good outcomes. Coupled with this is the important differentiation between "service providers", who perform a specified task, and "advisors", who have the skills and ability to provide guidance and assistance, beyond a basic service. Failing to appreciate these differences represents a significant risk to business owners.

The bookkeeper of the future, therefore, is someone who can "reverse engineer" all of these electronic transactions that are occurring at mach speed, bringing knowledge and insight to their work, while ensuring that the burden of proof is properly met with the CRA and *that only the correct amount of tax is remitted, and no more.* The "old fashioned" notion of the burden of proof is not disappearing anytime soon, and in fact, with more sophisticated artificial intelligence, new technological advances will give CRA even greater powers to audit, question, and disrupt a business owner's control of cash flow.

A bookkeeper must also understand the integration of personal and corporate tax systems, as well as the business and accounting related systems and procedures that connect with the flow of money between banking and government. Coupled with this is the necessity to precisely pinpoint and explain transactions in relation to the financial statements that are presented to business owners for decision-making purposes. More analysis and discussion, *from the business owner's point of view*, is typically required, given that financial planning begins with how much money is in the bank, what is left after all obligations are satisfied, and how this residual amount is going to be further invested, for use by people or the company.

To this end, a *DFA-Bookkeeping Services Specialist*™[3] is a designated professional trained to work in a multi-stakeholder environment, including the business owner and other professionals, such as CPAs, financial advisors, and lawyers. This ability is critical for filling the gap that business owners so often encounter.

Developing a multi-stakeholder approach to long term planning. Consider the stakeholders of a tax-wise financial continuity plan, as illustrated below. The Real Wealth Manager™[4] is the trusted advisor who develops a strategic wealth management plan with the professional advisory team—specialists in personal, corporate, and cross-border taxation; various financial and insurance specialists; legal and business advisors; in consultation with the Chief Family Influencer or CFI. This is the person

3 This professional has earned this designation by studying a rigorous 18-month competency program, available from Knowledge Bureau.

4 This professional has earned the RWM designation, available from Knowledge Bureau.

who manages the family stakeholders to the plan. Together, these two catalysts make it their business to follow through on the plans that will ensure the best financial outcomes and peace of mind for both the company and the family.

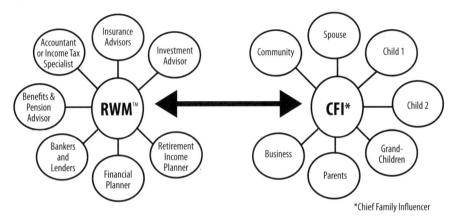

*Chief Family Influencer

Getting the Tax Right. Getting all of the stakeholders together to develop a strategic family financial plan is no easy task. The catalyst is the Chief Family Influencer—likely you, if you are reading this book. This is the person that the family turns to for financial guidance and support; the one who likely assembles and is responsible for preparing the family's tax returns, or ensures that everyone is reminded about these obligations. This is also often the person who might take on responsibilities such as Power of Attorney or Executor, when disability or death occur.

The annual trigger, and most important financial document that family members engage on a regular basis, is the requirement to file a tax return. With this requirement comes the need to assemble annual income, investment results, and opportunities, as individuals, as a couple, and as a coordinated family unit, all poised to take advantage of the tax preferences that CRA has to offer.

So, how do you assemble the right team to get the desired financial results and control the tax risk that business owners constantly face? Few tax and financial advisors have all the necessary skills to manage a financial plan over a lengthy timeline; however, there are seven big opportunities for business owners and their family members to discuss with their advisors, as itemized below.

This list also provides a great interview guide when choosing your professional advisory team. Ask them how they would work with your family unit to engage in the following areas. Doing so will provide quick insight into whether or not the person in front of you has the knowledge and skills to help, as well as if they have a specialized network to support their efforts:

- **Income Diversification.** Especially if the enterprise is incorporated, understanding the right mix of salary, dividends, and bonuses to create the optimum annual income level for owners and family members—active or non-active—is a critical first step to taking advantage of the right tax planning opportunities. Discuss the following questions with your tax specialist:

  - How much employment income must be drawn in order to maximize Canada Pension Plan contributions to fund future CPP disability or retirement benefits?

  - How much employment income must be drawn in order to maximize Registered Retirement Savings Plan contributions?

  - How much retained earnings does the company require in order to distribute dividends to the owner and the family members, for investment in Tax Free Savings Accounts that are held personally?

- **Split Income with Family Members.** A family that works together in a business could significantly reduce taxes that are payable by the family unit as a whole, but tax rules and restrictions could limit these opportunities. Answering the following questions could provide helpful resolution:

  - Could family members who are working in the family business be paid a salary or a bonus?

  - How much are the new taxes on dividends that are distributed to family members who are not actively involved in the business[5]?

  - Is it possible to avoid tax rules on split income upon retirement?

- **Invest with Gross Income.** Invest "first dollars earned" back into the business. This could lengthen the investment period, and depending on the type of investments chosen, result in a deferral of taxes on investment earnings, culminating in a larger nest egg in the future. These investment opportunities take advantage of the

---

5 For an overview of the new Tax on Split Income rules, effective January 1, 2018, see the Appendix to this book.

time value of money; that is, income earning capacity is exponentially increased by investing sooner rather than later. This privilege of working with first dollars earned is unavailable to employees. Their employers are required, by law, to submit first dollars earned to governments by way of withholding taxes—usually over-deducted, without paying interest. This is at the great expense of precious investment time lost by taxpayers, who must also wait for their tax refunds well into the next calendar year.

However, for the business owner, this privilege to use gross dollars comes at a cost: risk management. Most business owners must have money in the bank before any financial institution will lend to finance fluctuating cash flows of a business. Retained earnings must be held on hand to fund future expansion, too. But now, aside from market volatility and unpredictable returns, these investments in private corporations face even more risks to their purchasing power: increased taxes.

Significant retained earnings in a private corporation that produce passive investment income are subject to new tax rules, effective January 1, 2019. These rules will restrict access to the preferential tax rates enjoyed by small business corporations when passive investment earnings exceed $50,000. This tax change certainly brings with it a blow to growth-oriented initiatives in new market innovation, as taxes on active business income increase.

Larger, growing enterprises will, therefore, want to manage investments earned in the corporation carefully. Consultation with an experienced tax specialist who understands both the new rules and how to transition funds within existing structures and investments, so as to experience the least amount of harm to the family's overall wealth management plan, is critical.

Despite these setbacks, with proper planning, the opportunity to invest a corporation's retained earnings still provides a significant benefit, to shore up borrowing needs and build retirement income funds. Dividends that are distributed in retirement by active shareholders who have reached the age of 65 to non-active family members, ultimately, can be distributed without limitation. This is an advantage over income splitting rules with employer-sponsored pensions or privately funded Registered Retirement Savings Plans where an election to split up to 50% of qualifying pension income sources puts a cap on tax savings. Again, tax planning with a highly qualified retirement income specialist[6] is recommended.

- **Consume with business dollars.** Business owners can write off the business portion of personal expenses, but never the personal portion. However, because the company buys consumables with lower-taxed dollars, there is an inherent advantage to having the business fund mixed-use expenses.

- **Time income and equity distributions carefully.** A multi-stakeholder, family approach to tax planning could help to average down tax costs for each individual over a period of years by controlling the timing of income sources: salary, dividends, and capital gains from the disposition of business investments, and ultimately, the company itself. Good financial communication within the family stakeholder group is critical to generate the right results.

- **Use the Lifetime Capital Gains Exemption (LCGE).** By building value in the goodwill, shareholdings, and other corporate assets, families could exponentially increase their terminal wealth. Recall that both individuals and businesses have lifecycles. There is a deemed disposition upon the death of a human taxpayer that could result in taxable capital gains being generated. Simplistically, this could be avoided with a tax-free rollover to a spouse, but in the case of a qualifying enterprise, it is possible to take advantage of a lucrative lifetime capital gains exemption available to each qualifying individual through a variety of tax planning strategies that could be put into place during one's lifetime. This is an important area to discuss with your tax and financial advisors, as at the time of publication, this provision had escaped the tax knife, providing a tax free exemption of $1 Million for qualifying farmers and fishers, and close to $870,000 for other qualifying small business corporations.

- **Leave a substantial financial legacy.** Bolster tax-advantaged dividend distributions and the lifetime capital gains exemption with tax free life insurance proceeds, funded by low-rate corporate dollars. This strategy is also a great way to ensure the continuity of management within a company, when the lifecycle of the owners ends before that of the business.

- **Manage debt and audit activity.** Business owners must bear all of the risk for delivering the product and/or services that result in

6 Professionals with the MFA-Retirement & Succession Services Specialist Designation can be of assistance with specialized skills.

income; and sometimes, must face the disappointment of incurring bad debts. Start-up losses do average out future taxes payable, as they can be carried back and applied to income in previous and future years, depending on the business' structure. Harvesting them wisely for future use is important; as is preserving the use of capital cost allowances (CCA) that are allowed on depreciable assets. (Please refer to the Appendix for recent tax changes that speed up tax benefits for asset acquisitions). These tax provisions provide important tools to use when the CRA tax auditor comes along. By keeping other creditors current and happy, business owners buy important time to pay for unexpected audit results that could drain cash flow swiftly, especially as CRA has the power to garnishee bank accounts and wages.

Managing Increased Audit Activity. The government has been increasingly concerned about the "tax gap" emerging from the underground economy and offshore tax havens. Recent budgets have allocated $1 Billion to shore up CRA resources and sophistication in combatting tax evasion, increasing verification and tax collection activities, hiring additional auditors, and developing robust business intelligence infrastructure. This investment is expected to address the billions of dollars CRA estimates it is losing to the "tax gap": assessed taxes not collected estimated to be more than $2 Billion and taxes related to unreported income estimated to be over $6 billion, for a combined tax gap of just under $9 billion.[7]

What this means to business owners is three things: (i) tax enforcement and collection is a much bigger priority for government; (ii) there is little patience for delinquent taxpayers; and (iii) looking forward, enough "grey areas" have been inserted into new tax laws, that new uncertainty has been introduced for business owners, their family members, and their financial advisors. Always, the burden of proof is on the taxpayer to justify claims on a tax return that is submitted to the CRA. Now, that burden of proof has been transferred to recipients of distributed income sources from the business, who may face recharacterization of income in future tax audits, and with that, top rate taxation.

The *Income Tax Act* is, in fact, is mostly silent on what deductions can be claimed by the self-employed taxpayer, simply stating that a taxpayer's income for the year from a business or property is the taxpayer's "profit" thereon. Even this term is not defined in the Act, but one can be sure that an outlay or expense will only be legitimate if it has a business purpose, as deduction of personal expenditures is expressly prohibited.

---

7 April 24, 2018, Tax Assured and Tax Gap for the Federal Personal Income Tax System, CRA.

Under Section 67 of the Act, for example, it specifically states that a deduction must be reasonable under the circumstances. And, under Section 18, a deduction must be made for the purpose of gaining or producing income from the business or property. However, what this also means is that unless an expenditure is specifically restricted or prohibited by the Income Tax Act, and if it is reasonable in the circumstances and incurred for the purpose of producing business income, it is deductible.

While CRA has the distinct advantage of hindsight in judging what is reasonable under the circumstances, a business owner has the distinct advantage of describing the circumstances faced in anticipating future revenues, at the time the financial decision was made. Whether or not profits actually resulted is not the issue; it is the fact the expenditures were made for the purposes of producing business income that matters. Business owners, in other words, have the advantage of *foresight*... and that's important when appealing CRA's audit activities. But, it's critical that all of the proper documentation is provided and tax compliance obligations are followed.

Understanding this powerplay becomes especially important with new tax rules on family income splitting, under which the concept of "reasonableness" was reintroduced by CRA. As mentioned, this begets a climate of uncertainty likely to result in at least a few precedent-setting court battles in the future from which to draw guidance, as business owners and CRA fight for their respective positions.

Looking forward, therefore, to a world in which family business ownership is increasingly under tax scrutiny, a number of basic tax issues should be discussed with your inter-generational family stakeholders and multi-stakeholder professional team (particularly, your tax specialists):

- Are all family members prepared for increased CRA scrutiny with proper documentation?

- Is it still possible to diversify and split income in the family and what audit risks would you now face?

- Who faces the burden of proof: the business owners or the family members who have received either employment or dividend income from the entity? Remember that under new rules *the burden of proof has shifted from the business owner, who distributes the money, in particular dividends, to the family members who report it on their personal tax returns.*

- And finally, does it still make sense to accumulate passive investment income in a private corporation, and if so, what financial planning strategies should the business owner consider in making investment decisions?

Not only are these important areas to consider as part of the transition of tax rules, but also in terms of a family business' ongoing strategy.

SUMMARY: DEFUSING THE FAMILY BUSINESS TIME BOMB

Minefields

- When it comes to managing the risks we know, it may seem likely that the uncertainty of the markets and tax changes work against us. But good information on tax and economic projections available from the Finance Department can help. Be sure to read about them in the annual Federal Budget and the Fall Economic Statement.

- Managing risks that pertain to the future earnings potential of the investment in the family business is critical. Putting gross income to work in the company or in wisely chosen financial assets matters a lot. But even more so, a careful vigilance is required to preserve the biggest investment family business owners have: the value of their equity in the company itself. It makes so much sense, therefore, to fortify the foundations and strength of that asset against the big wealth eroders: the taxes payable on income throughout an owner's personal lifecycle and later, upon the transition of the asset to others, by sale or transfer.

- Managing risks of all sorts requires foresight, process, and discipline, to mitigate damage that might occur in the future. In mitigating risks to human health, for example, proactive and preventative measures could be implemented to identify and evaluate risks and proactively reduce them. Likewise, risks to financial health involve the unknown—market disruptors, tax changes, and retroactive tax audit, which always casts a cloud of uncertainty over a sound go-forward business plan. On an ongoing basis, prevent whatever damage you could reasonably predict with sound personal and financial health practices. Then, work with trusted and knowledgeable tax specialists, as thoroughly as you would with your heart specialist or oncologist.

Tools

- Find the right advisors. Their good work will pay off, starting with the quality of the work your knowledgeable and diligent bookkeeping professionals bring to your day-to-day financial and documentation requirements, to the specialists that really understand ancient and emerging tax laws that coincide with the lifecycles of both the business and the humans who work in it.

- By finding and engaging the right multi-advisory professional team, they will check each other's knowledge, skills, and expertise against your financial goals and aspirations for yourself and your business. Many minds, all bringing their best skills to work towards the same strategy for your future, in other words, are powerful. Then, go out and build your company and your family's wealth by doing what you do so brilliantly.

- Fight for your Taxpayer Rights. Under our self-assessment system of taxation, it is your legal right to arrange your affairs according to the laws that are in force at the time you do so, in order to pay the least amount of taxes legally possible. You must pay the correct amount of tax, on time, but not one cent more. The Taxpayer Bill of Rights is an interesting read—there are 16 of them—and five commitments, specifically to Small Business. Amongst them:

    o "The Canada Revenue Agency (CRA) is committed to administering the tax system in a way that minimizes the cost of compliance for small business.

    o The CRA is committed to working with all governments to streamline service, minimize cost, and reduce the compliance burden.

    o The CRA is committed to explaining how we conduct our business with small business."

You and your powerful team of tax and financial specialists can hold CRA to their commitments to you.

YOUR MISSION: Managing the Risks We Know—Taxes Really Matter.

READY **THINGS YOU NEED TO KNOW**

- The onus of proof for all the financial affairs of the business is on the owner and the family members who receive any form of compensation from the company. All family members must be counselled to know and understand these risks.

- Family business owners, both incorporated and unincorporated, must be prepared to make a variety of tax remittances and ensure that sufficient cash flow is on hand to stay onside with the CRA: from GST/HST, to payroll, to income tax prepayments. Failure to file and remit to the CRA is expensive and this demanding "partner" in your business has the power to seize your receivables, income, and assets and hold your Directors responsible for source remittances.

- Income splitting with the family is still possible, but only by meeting CRA's now much more onerous compliance criteria. It has always been necessary to show the taxman that the family member you are paying is doing work that would have been done by a stranger, for the same remuneration (must be reasonable for the amount and nature of the role) and that you actually paid and remitted source deductions, as required. Be sure to pay periodically by cheque or electronic deposit, but if cash is paid, have the family member sign a receipt, acknowledging the payment.

  In addition, before distributing dividends from a private corporation, it is necessary to show a reasonable contribution of time, talent and/or capital, to avoid top-rate taxation. Detailed documentation is also required.

- It is still possible to build significant wealth by being self-employed, however. Lower corporate tax rates continue to leave behind bigger corporate dollars for the purposes of re-investment and investment earnings within a corporate entity grow faster, as a result. Income splitting is more advantageous too, provided that a spouse that is actively involved in the business has reached age 65.

- How have recent tax reforms affected the planning I need to do for my business?

- How can I plan to avoid trouble with the CRA in the future, by shoring up new documentation requirements?

- Is the Lifetime Capital Gains Exemption still available to our family?

- Does it still make sense to have a holding company and/or a family trust?

- When is the right time to plan to take a steady stream of dividends from the company for retirement purposes?

- What will happen to investments in the corporation and the assets in the company, from a tax point of view, upon the key shareholder's death?

THINGS YOU NEED TO DO

- Review your business structure with your tax accountant and lawyer and co-ordinate investment activities with the tax obstacles that are now in place.

- Review your life insurance coverage to see whether some investments should be held there to avoid new tax rules, and to be sure that there are no liquidity problems upon the death of the business owners.

DEFUSE DECISIONS YOU NEED TO MAKE

- What are the effects of tax changes on the cash flow of the business? Determine whether they are significant enough to affect the operations and if so, how this should be addressed.

- Think about your retirement income plan, in terms of how to split income with your spouse and when.

- Discuss the continuity of the business should there be a disposition, and what the tax consequences would be in this event.

✔ **Mission Accomplished:** The resources that are invested to grow a family business have a lifecycle, and this applies to two basic categories: the returns achieved from the investment of human capital and those received from the investment of financial capital. The CRA is increasingly interested in tracking any tax advantages that may be achieved by the family unit, both inside and outside the corporate entity. This is a problem that arises from the fact that it is the individual, rather than the family economic unit, that is the subject of taxation in Canada. It is possible that future comprehensive tax reforms could address this.

However, in the meantime, it is this continuum of efforts by people and money, individuals and corporations, that must be tracked in order to get the best after-tax results and to defend the health of the business and its dependants from new tax risks.

Now is a good time to discuss cash flow, retirement, and estate planning with you knowledgeable team of professional financial advisors, working in collaboration with the entire family in an integrated wealth management approach.

9

Tax Consequences of Business Disposition
Getting the Best Results

Nothing is certain, but death and taxes, as the saying goes. Ian always chuckled when his accountant reliably uttered this ancient phrase, as he shrugged in his enduring way, each and every tax season. Ian had been very lucky, as he would tell his friends. Yes, he had worked very hard all of his life, with many trials along the way, as his business ebbed and flowed with both the obstacles and the miracles that come with the territory. He was appreciative, too, for the stellar professional financial team he had assembled.

But today, he was visiting his accountant mid-year, with a frown. He had a new glimpse into the future that morning and now knew something that he really preferred not to tell anyone: he was diagnosed with Stage 3 cancer—quite a shock—and now, the first person he would consult about it would be his long time tax advisor. Perhaps it was a rehearsal for what was to come next: breaking the news to his wife of 30 years and his two grown children.

The reality of estate planning, he realized, as he and his accountant locked head and heart, was that it's never really meaningful—and is something that is easy to put off—until the shock of human frailty is on display before you. Deathbed planning is not a good addition to the stress of fighting for one's health and it is always best accomplished when everyone in the family is healthy.

However, there was some good news for Ian. The two men spent some time discussing the lucrative Lifetime Capital Gains Exemption, for those who own a qualifying Canadian Controlled Private Corporation, as Ian did. They put all the checks and balances into place to allow for the nuances of continuity planning that would be tax effective, should Ian's illness progress more quickly than expected. Together, they had approached the certainty of taxes and pitted all of their planning tools against the uncertain timeline that the inevitability of death brought with it. This was, indeed, a relief for Ian.

In the meantime, he faced a more immediate tax challenge: Ian had accumulated a healthy nest-egg of retained earnings that was generating a substantive amount of passive investment earnings. He had always been concerned about rising interest rates and his ability to finance corporate needs, but now, he needed to be the catalyst for the interim financial plan—the one that would take his family and his business from his capacity to incapacity, and onward to a new stage, ultimately, without him.

THE ISSUES

Family business owners have many options to consider in contemplating business succession planning. It is a matter that many, in fact, consider over a long period of time; yet inaction is a hallmark of the process for a variety of reasons, the top[8] ones being:

- Finding a suitable successor
- Valuing the business
- Too much dependence on owner-manager's involvement
- Financing the successor
- Starting and developing a succession plan
- Access to cost-effective professional advice
- Conflicting business vision of family members or employees
- Business succession is not a priority

All of these reasons for inertia are important; however, it is likely the last one that is the most important. When business succession is not a priority—for whatever reason—risk management relating to human capital or financial wealth cannot be mitigated.

We have learned that amongst the biggest risks to financial health of people and business enterprises is the uncertainty of tax audit and abrupt changes in tax laws. Transfer of ownership in a business potentially has a variety of tax consequences, depending upon whether it is gifted, sold, or simply wound down. The consequences also differ, depending upon the structure: proprietorship, partnership, or corporation. They could also differ with other choices: for example, the opportunity for mergers or acquisitions of other firms, at some point in the business lifecycle. Any of these options requires a "run up" time and a long ramp of transition, before the next incarnation of business ownership can be successfully launched.

Regardless of the tax options, the first order of business in succession planning is to ensure that an up-to-date will, Power of Attorney, and health care directive are all in place. These represent the important legal documents that allow you to have control over your financial affairs, when you cannot be the one to provide direction.

8 CFIB Survey, Getting the Transition Right, November 2018

No one likes to discuss the real human frailties of disability and death, but we have all heard stories of family conflict about money and inheritance that have destroyed communication between siblings, children, and grandchildren. Sadly, we all know of predatory behaviors from people who are close to those family leaders, who now suffer from dementia and other chronic illnesses. While taxes and inflation are major eroders of a lifetime of careful asset accumulation, legal fees spent to quell family discord could be just as devasting to the family's net worth. It is a critical part of a family wealth management strategy to plan for financial continuity when the Chief Family Influencer is stricken and no longer able to bring leadership to this important role.

Fortunately, the annual tax filing requirement is an effective trigger for family discussion about the inevitability of death. It is possible to transfer assets during one's lifetime to get the best overall tax results upon death. It is also possible to equalize an estate with life insurance and other tax-efficient structures to protect family members from each other's emotionally-challenged decision-making after the business and/or family leader becomes ill or passes away.

The Bottom Line: The eventual disposition of a company, and its transition over to new owners, no matter who they might be, is the single most important responsibility of a successful business owner. The stewardship of all of that wealth—after tax—to ensure a successful legacy that will continue to create economic growth, jobs for people in the community, and returns on investment of the owner, cannot be a slip-shod, unplanned process.

It all begins with an understanding that the business itself is a significant capital asset that derives its value from the income produced by those who work in it; but also from the savvy strategic moves the owners make to ensure its healthy assent—year over year, generation after generation. Family businesses that do this well survive generations.

But, you must be aware of the tax consequences. Unlike the lifecycle of a human, which has a definitive end, a corporate or trust structure could continue to live on, and bear fruit, for many years to come. Accrued gains on the cost base of assets are generally subject to taxation on a transfer of ownership. Losses in the value of assets have tax consequences, too, and although often a setback, there is value even in a tax loss, which can offset taxes payable for many years to come. What is most critical to this is proper planning.

THE SOLUTIONS

For all of the issues identified, expert tax and business valuation advice is required along the way; preferably, something that is addressed annually in your tax filing and compliance discussions with your tax specialist. There may be several important questions to consider:

- What is the company worth, based on our current revenue and profitability levels? What is it expected to be worth at the end of the current business cycle?

- How much should we invest—and where—to shore up our predicted business valuation in the near future?

- Should the right opportunity for merger, acquisition or partnership emerge in the foreseeable future, is the business well-positioned to embrace it, or will we be leaving money on the table?

- Is there insurance to cover the liabilities that would occur upon the death of key individuals in the company?

- Who currently owns shares in the business? Who should own them and what percentage of votes and value need to be owned in order to meet family income splitting tests and benefit from the LCGE (Lifetime Capital Gains Exemption)?

- Should these assets, alternatively, pass through to the beneficiaries of a discretionary family trust?

You have learned the answers to some of these questions in the last chapter. But, it is important to continuously probe, to get new answers based on changing conditions in the marketplace, ensuring crystallization of the value in the business, either during your lifetime, or at death, and to take advantage of generous tax opportunities like the LCGE, too.

Disposition of Private Corporation Shares. When the shares of a qualifying Small Business Corporation are disposed, it is possible for *individual shareholders* to benefit from the Lifetime Capital Gains Exemption (LCGE). The value of this exemption was just under $900,000 at the time of writing and is expected to drift up with inflation to the $1 Million amount that is currently allowed to qualifying farm property owners. There are three types of qualifying properties:

- Certain small business corporations
- Certain qualifying farm and fishing properties

- For any of the dispositions above, reserves that are brought into income.

It is also possible for Lifetime Capital Gains Exemptions to be designated to beneficiaries of discretionary family trusts. However, it's important to discuss what recent tax changes can impact these structures and how to structure the best after-tax outcomes during the owner's lifetime. Details about the calculation of the exemption can be found in the Appendix to this book.

Most owners would prefer to sell shares in order to benefit from the LCGE. When shares of the business are sold, all of the company's liabilities are transferred to the new owner. As a result, the new ownership might prefer to "cherry pick" the best assets, transfer them to a new or existing enterprise, and leave you with the shares and associated liabilities, and without access to the LCGE for each shareholder in the family. For these reasons, business owners often prefer to take control of the LCGE, to ensure that the family benefits from value that has been accrued in the company to date.

Estate Freezes. A common way to maximize family wealth and the LCGE is to initiate an estate freeze, ensuring that future gains in the company would be taxed in the hands of the taxpayer's beneficiaries. In this scenario, the value of the estate is determined at the time of the freeze, and so is the tax. This can enable the use of the LCGE on a future sale. If the "freeze" shares are still held at the date of death planning should be done to be sure funds are present to pay taxes at death. By knowing this, a taxpayer could take steps to acquire life insurance, as an example, to provide a source of funds to be used to pay taxes upon their death. There are many ways to accomplish an estate freeze, which should be discussed with an experienced professional.

The future growth in the company could also be transferred to a discretionary family trust, whose beneficiaries would be the intended heirs. This approach provides some additional security, as it separates beneficial ownership from legal ownership, thereby protecting the estate from creditors or claims by other family members.

When a taxpayer has frozen the value of shares under an estate freeze, it is also possible to redeem the fixed value of the shares over time, as a form of retirement income. This would reduce the tax consequences of a deemed disposition at death, and if this strategy is employed over time, taxes could be averaged down and minimized.

It is important to recognize, however, that stripping too much cash out of a company could put it at financial risk, and potentially, at risk of an unfavorable tax audit. It could also cause family strife.

A Will for the Business—Estate Equalization. Most family businesses include active and non-active family members; they could also be blessed with non-related, but key employees who diligently work on the growth of income in the company and the stewardship of its assets into the future.

Astute business owners recognize the need to put sound legal documentation into place, ensuring that each of the key stakeholders in the company and family group are addressed in the estate planning documents. If this is done while the owner-manager is healthy, life insurance could be obtained to equalize the estate for all family members: those who are active in the business, and those who are not; those who use the family cottage, and those who cannot; those who are financially stable vs. those who are not.

Most importantly, by avoiding family strife over money and assets and managing the risk of future tax changes, the care of a vulnerable spouse or loved one could be more confidently arranged and provided.

Other Asset Dispositions. A business usually has acquired other assets along the way, such as, depreciable items that are consumed over the course of producing income—machinery and equipment, for example—as well as an inventory of items that are sold for profit, and in some cases, intangible assets.

Intangible assets are important. These are assets that might not have a tangible or physical presence that is separable and licensable—such as intellectual property, trademarks, brand names, domain names, certification marks, non-compete agreements, franchise agreements, leases, royalties, patents, permits, know-how, customer lists, and goodwill—all of which require valuation when there is a change in ownership.

This represents an important issue that could be championed now, during your healthy lifetime, especially in the case of a technology or information-based business or one that earns significant revenue from its intellectual property. When these assets are identified, valued, and protected, they could add quite significantly to a company's value; a relatively new phenomenon in the digital age and one that should not be forgotten in your planning efforts.

Characteristics of Dispositions. It is also important to understand that dispositions of any business could be voluntary or involuntary. An example of a voluntary disposition is the deliberate sale or winding down of an unincorporated enterprise or the implementation of an estate freeze for a private corporation. These options are usually taken under the control of the owners, with a wind-up obviously being less attractive than a sale at the right price.

An involuntary disposition occurs at death, or when there is a another "deemed disposition"; examples include an expropriation or foreclosure, or when business assets are transferred. Because no money changes hands at the time, valuation at Fair Market Value (FMV) is required for tax purposes. This is the highest price that could be obtained for the business in an open market, between an unrelated buyer and a seller, and is how the tax consequences are generated: (i) the actual proceeds received upon sale; or (ii) the FMV on a deemed disposition on a specific date.

There are several sections of the Income Tax Act that govern deemed dispositions, but of the most important to business owners is typically S. 69 (gifting of property), S. 70(5) (death of the owner), and S. 104(4), which invokes a deemed disposition of the capital property held in a trust every 21 years. Ask your tax advisors to explain the implications of each section and their appropriate use and timing, according to your specific financial goals and opportunities.

Non-arm's length transactions. When related people deal with one other—for example, when children inherit or purchase capital property from parents—they are considered to be dealing at non-arm's length. When transactions occur that exceed or are below FMV (known as "inadequate consideration"), penalties could occur. This could be really problematic, if Mom and Dad sell their company to a child for nominal value. Consider the following rules:

- where a taxpayer acquires a property from a related person for an amount that is more than FMV, the cost of the property is deemed to be the FMV. This rule eliminates the ability to "bump" up the cost base of a property by transferring it to a related party at more than its FMV. Note that the vendor will still account for proceeds of disposition that are greater than FMV, as there is no provision in the Act to mirror this reduction to cost. Therefore, double taxation results.

- where a taxpayer disposes of property to a related person for an amount that is less than FMV, the taxpayer will have deemed proceeds of disposition equal to the FMV. This removes the potential avoidance of income or capital gain on the transfer of the property.

Unfortunately again there is no mechanism to have the cost increased to Fair Market Value in the hands of the related party. Therefore, there is the possibility of double taxation.

Another important rule to observe is as follows: a terminal loss on the transfer of depreciable property would not be recognized in a non-arm's length transaction. Terminal losses occur when there is more depreciation in the value of an asset than has been recorded on the books. This generally results in a tax deduction against income earned; except when it occurs on non-arm's length transactions... again, an unfavorable and expensive tax result.

Weighing the Options. Many business leaders have the idea that their company will ultimately be passed to the next generation of their family; perhaps, this is a romantic notion that transcends the enterprise itself. It's important to remember that this might not be the case for a range of reasons, which means that business owners should consider their options on an ongoing basis.

There are tax implications in every situation, be it a wind-down, a sale, merger, new shareholder, reorganization, raising capital, or anything in between, so be sure to have experienced tax and business advisors alongside throughout your tenure. These professionals can help to identify options and recommend favourable courses of action, as well as advise as to the specific tax circumstances of each situation. The benefit of doing so is that you will be ready to take action when needed, in a situation where timing could be everything.

You may be interested in learning more about the tax implications of succession planning. A good place to start is with the tax and wealth management courses offered online by Knowledge Bureau. The pre-eminent education provider to thousands of tax and financial advisors throughout Canada, these courses provide a unique opportunity for business owners to come up to speed with the issues to be discussed and the variety of tax-savings options available when long term planning is embarked upon.

After the Disposition—A New Business? Despite all of the risks and tax pitfalls, it is not unusual for successful business owners to start again after the disposition of a company. A special tax provision, called the Replacement Property Rules, may be used to defer taxes into the future. Here is how it works:

If a taxpayer receives proceeds from the disposition of property (other than shares) and later replaces that property, within 24 months after the end of the year of disposition, in the case of an involuntary disposition, or 12 months after the end of a voluntary disposition, it is possible to defer any resulting capital gain or recaptured depreciation.

To accomplish this, a taxpayer files the tax return on the basis that the election has been made in the year in which the former company was disposed, or by requesting an adjustment to a prior filed return, if the new business was acquired in a year after the original disposition. Speak to your tax advisor about this provision and how it could be applied to your circumstances.

SUMMARY: DEFUSING THE FAMILY BUSINESS TIME BOMB

Minefields

There are a few new tax terms that family business owners need to master in order to fully maximize their tax-free capital gains on the sale or transfer of their company:

- Ask your tax specialist about CNIL. The Cumulative Net Investment Loss (CNIL) rules could prevent you from claiming the Lifetime Capital Gains Exemption on the sale or disposition of your qualifying small business corporation's shares. A CNIL could arise where you have borrowed money and deducted interest on funds advanced to your company. Review your tax filings with your accountant prior to closing on a sale.

- Find out about the Alternative Minimum Tax (AMT). This provision could apply to create taxes owing in the year of sale, arising because of a special tax calculation that excludes tax preference items, such as the Lifetime Capital Gains Exemption.

- Learn more about TOSI—Tax on Split Income—and the new rules behind the taxation of passive investments in a private corporation. Corporate taxation is rising, but astute planning can help.

Tools

- Act sooner rather than later. When an offer to acquire your company emerges, it might be too late to restructure and fix an "offside" corporate structure. If you have to wait 24 months before the shares qualify again, the buyer will likely have long since moved on.

- Assess your risk for capital gains taxes. An untimely death or disposition could result in an unexpected capital gains tax. For this reason, it is prudent for the company to carry adequate life insurance to fund an unexpected tax liability. This is easier and less expensive the healthier you are.

- Review your will to ensure that you understand the tax consequences that could arise on a transfer of property occurring upon death. While a transfer to a spouse or spousal trust occurs on a tax-deferred rollover basis, generally speaking, a transfer to your children does not. Such a transfer could trigger an unexpected capital gains tax, which could destabilize the business or your other investments.

- Seek competent tax advice. These matters are extremely complex, the rules are new, and the onus of proof and compliance is on you and your heirs.

YOUR MISSION: Tax Consequences of Business Disposition. Getting the Best Results.

READY THINGS YOU NEED TO KNOW

- As an owner of a private corporation, your shares probably represent a significant percentage of your net worth. It's important to consider a succession plan, from a tax point of view, preferably with every tax return that is filed. How much potential tax would be payable if something were to happen to you? Are you insured to cover the taxes payable? What other options are available?

- You, and each and every family member, could be entitled to the Lifetime Capital Gains Exemption. Be sure to structure shareholdings to maximize this lucrative tax advantage. The tests under the Income Tax Act to ensure that the shares of the family business qualify are complex: there is a 50% "24-month test", a 90% "substantially-all test" at the date of sale, and new rules where there is a Holdco-Opco structure. Speak to your tax and legal advisors annually to ensure that you are onside with these rules when planning for sale or succession.

- A family trust is still an excellent way to multiply the Lifetime Capital Gains Exemption. The trust could also provide flexibility and creditor-proofing for the family as a whole.

- Work on understanding what would be left, after tax, for your retirement lifestyle, given new tax rules on passive investment income earned in your company. Is your nest-egg too big? Will it cause high taxation on your active business income? Should you distribute more income into your personal hands now and continue your investment strategy there?

SET QUESTIONS YOU NEED TO ASK

- What is your company worth today?

- Have you included intangibles—intellectual property ownership—in the value calculations?

- When do you plan to sell or transfer ownership?

- Do you have a successor in mind? Have you told him or her of your plans?

- Do the shares that you or your family members own qualify for the Lifetime Capital Gains Exemption?

- How much tax would have to be paid if you sold today?

- Is it likely that your children or employees would want to buy the company?

- What issues would arise in the family if some children wanted to buy, but others didn't?

- What issues would arise with employees, in this case?

- What would happen to the company if you were suddenly disabled?

- Have you ensured that your business could continue to grow, after tax, with or without you? What additional safeguards would you put into place, if you could not answer yes to this question?

THINGS YOU NEED TO DO

- Assess the current estimated value of your company.

- Identify tax strategies to minimize tax on active earnings today.

- Identify strategies to minimize tax on a future sale (or transfer to other family members).

- Review the corporate structure with a view to maximizing overall family wealth, despite new tax changes for family income splitting and the earning of passive investment income in the company.

- Review your personal investments, pensions, and other income sources that provide you with taxable earnings and assess how and when you wish to take a regular income in the form of non-eligible dividends. Could any of these receipts be deferred or sped up to average taxes downward over the rest of your lifecycle? Could any of these income sources be split with your spouse or family members?

- Assess your eligibility to claim the Lifetime Capital Gains Exemption, and do so for every family member, every year.

- Do you need to restructure your corporate holdings?

- Should you consider adding a family trust?

- Should you consider the use of a holding company?

- Should you revisit your salary/dividend mix?

- Should you revisit your investment strategies for capital held inside and outside of your corporation?

- From a retirement planning perspective, does it make sense to distribute dividends to your spouse once you reach age 65, and if so, how much should be received each year?

✔ **Mission Accomplished:** When family business owners properly structure their affairs surrounding the ownership of their corporate asset, significant long-term wealth could be built for current and future generations. It pays to get specialized tax advice, in advance and throughout your tenure.

10

Defusing the Family Business Time Bomb for Real:
Legacy Matters

We have all heard the heartbreaking stories of the Mega Rich: from recent situations in Canada, to countless famous families in business, entertainment, and politics in the United States and around the world. The common threads include some familiar themes: too much money, power, privilege, or entitlement, in stark contrast to feelings of inequity, devasting betrayals, and unforgiving hurt, which tend to impact some more than others. This is a tragic way to end what has often been a life of hard work and dedication, leaving those who view these sagas from the outside to wonder "how could it have come to this?"

What if the story could have played out differently? One, instead, that fully appreciates and benefits from the opportunity to create a lasting and valuable legacy: a strong family tree, intertwined with a robust business venture that has the potential for health and prosperity for generations to come. Or, a family that has achieved success, stability, and harmony through building an exceptional company that was sold well, generating sufficient resources to pursue the next stage of life, and perhaps, contribute to the community as well. These represent admirable legacies.

There is big responsibility that comes with this notion of legacy. It begins with the shared values and goals, which by their very nature must be articulated, captured, and reinforced. Communication is the first common thread to a successful family culture and is something that cannot be underestimated. When a family can share its stories with all of the generations, as well as core beliefs in terms of how a personal and business life could be lived well, it is possible to develop a common purpose for each.

This shared purpose will inevitably be interrupted by many real life disruptors: births, deaths, marriages, divorces, great economic successes and setbacks, personal or business disability, and eventually, the death of one or more family members. It is in these moments when life can become truly difficult and it is a strong family culture that provides the necessary support to weather all of the "unthinkables", while enjoying the benefits, entitlements, and rewards that financial success can bring.

When a founder launches a business, it is often a blend of responding to a current need in the marketplace and dreams for the future. How far could my company go? Could my products and services be recognized as the best available someday? Would my children want to join the business? Could they be the next leaders and carry on the family name? Could selling my company fund my retirement? These dreams are often displaced by the all-consuming needs of the business, as each day passes, which can actually be more damaging than one might expect.

The biggest casualty? It is often the communications within the family unit—not just as a result of the absence of a strong and dynamic business founder to foster it, but in the ongoing silence of those who feel they will never be noticed, recognized, or heard, be it in the family or the company. To truly build and sustain a legacy, families need to be committed to a family code of conduct for the necessary planning and communication that sets the stage for pursuing opportunities in the future. *This is a great responsibility and should be seen as such by all of the stakeholders to the legacy.*

Given the brisk evolution of demographic, technological, and economic factors in today's new economy—an environment like no other—the failure to take an active, consistent, and strategic role in positioning a family business for future success is really not an option. When marketplace relevance, after-tax sustainability, and growing enterprise value are desired outcomes, it is critical that steps be taken to defuse the family business time bomb now.

Brave New You. Leadership Matters.

Successful family business leadership involves doing a number of important things well, with, perhaps, the first being able to have the *courage* to bring the stakeholders together under a common vision and strategic plan. Not just a halfhearted, kind of curious, musing interest, but rather, a commitment that is *all in*, to face and surpass whatever challenges are met along the way. This level of true courage and consistency is one that many business leaders do not take the time and effort to find, at the peril of the family legacy.

This is unfortunate, as there are many family businesses that have meaningful, long-term potential. Worse, in the absence of such courage, we have seen not only the sensational headlines of the fate of the ultra-rich, but also in the family enterprises in our communities, bringing permanent destruction to relationships between parents and their children, grandparents and their grandchildren, siblings and cousins. *This is a family and business legacy that no one wants.*

These tragic situations are characterized by companies that are not managed in a manner that creates the foundation for long term sustainability, of the business or the family's wealth, a responsibility that falls to the leadership role. And although some time might be granted to correct business shortfalls, this window is getting smaller each moment, as the world in which we live is evolving at an increasingly rapid and complex pace.

This ticking time bomb can be defused, however, by recognizing that making adjustments in alignment, to strategically position a company, is a continuous process that is required in order to remain relevant in the marketplace. This ongoing relevance sets the stage for attracting transition partners and value when the time comes and doing so can preserve the family culture and legacy as well, which is likely the most important outcome of all.

The new way forward will not just come from the founder's ongoing leadership, but rather the family's actions will determine whether or not their company has a future. Decisions that business leaders make today could have a profound impact on the company's ability to provide for the family's current income requirements, and future resources. Experienced professional advisors can be tremendously helpful to defusing the family business time bomb, ensuring that effective steps are taken to protect against loss of the significant effort that has been invested in building the company.

Your final Defuse mission is to find the time, strength, and yes, courage to take the necessary actions to protect your company—and all of your important stakeholder relationships—by ensuring that a sound transition plan is appropriately developed and positioned to meet the challenges of not only the current environment, but also for whatever the future might hold. *The good news? Taking on this important responsibility will bring with it priceless rewards.*

So, we leave you with this challenge: dig deep, dream big, defuse the issues that threaten the health of your company and family legacy, and then take the time to bask in the realization that you have done all that you can to build, grow, and transition from a position of strength. The peace of mind that comes with doing so is not only well worth the effort, it is something to celebrate!

Remember: finishing well matters.

Jenifer Bartman & Evelyn Jacks

APPENDIX

DEFUSING THE FAMILY BUSINESS TIME BOMB

FAMILY TAX PLANNING

Managing the complex tax rules that encompass the economic decisions made by a family—especially one that includes a family business—can be difficult, even for the advisors that help the family get the right tax results, throughout their lifetime and at the death of one or more of the individuals.

This appendix provides details on how CRA looks at family income splitting, both from the point of view of passive investment income earned personally and when family members work in the business.

These comments are designed to help focus discussions on the right opportunities to multiply family wealth against the risks inherent in managing a family business enterprise against the volatile financial markets in which it operates.

PERSONAL TAX CONSIDERATIONS

If the idea of transferring assets from the higher earner to the lower earners in the family seems too good to be true, it is. The result would be that tax on income is paid at the recipient's lower tax rates, leading to lower overall family taxes payable. CRA, however, frowns on such plans and will allow only limited income splitting. Here's what you need to know to make the right decisions with your professional advisory team:

The Attribution Rules. The transfer of assets from the higher earner to the lower earners in the family, so that tax on income is paid at lower tax brackets, is prohibited under the Income Tax Act, unless you properly hire your family members in the business, according to specific CRA rules, or meet certain exclusions or exceptions. The attribution rules prohibit the following transactions, specifically:

> • *Transfers and loans to spouse or common-law partner.* If you transfer or loan property either directly or indirectly, by means of a trust or any other means, to a spouse or common-law partner for that person's benefit, any resulting income or loss or

capital gain or loss from that property is taxable to you. In addition, where one spouse guarantees the repayment of a loan to the other spouse, made for investment purposes, attribution will apply to any income earned from the loaned funds.

- **Transfers and loans to minors.** Where property is transferred or loaned either directly or indirectly to a person who is under the age of 18 years and who does not deal with you at arm's length or who is your niece or nephew, the income or loss resulting from such property is reported by you until the transferee attains 18 years of age. Capital gains or losses do not, however, attribute back to you. In other words, income resulting from assets transferred to a minor child will trigger attribution of rental, dividend, or interest income, but not capital gains.

The Attribution Rules Can Be Avoided. There are several legal ways to get around the Attribution Rules, to legally engage in splitting income with family members. The following are examples:

- **Inheritances.** Attribution does not apply to inheritances. If possible, invest the money in separate savings accounts for the beneficiaries to verify the origin of the capital.

- **Tax-Free Savings Accounts.** If you make contributions to a Tax-Free Savings Account for your spouse or adult children, they will earn income on those deposits with no income tax payable, either by them or by you, so long as the contribution is a true gift and not a scheme to allow you to earn that income on a tax-free basis. These earnings will have no effect on your ability to claim the Spousal Amount.

- **Spousal RRSPs.** Attribution does not apply to contributions made to a spousal RRSP, unless there is a withdrawal within three years.

- **Interest income from Canada Child Benefit (CCB) payments.** If CCB payments are invested in the name of a child, the income will not be subject to attribution. In other words, interest, dividends, and other investment income may be reported in the hands of the child. Be sure this account remains untainted by birthday money and other gifts.

- **Joint accounts.** T5 Slips are issued by banks in the names of the account holders to report earnings on investments, including interest and dividends. This does not mean that the income on those slips is taxable to those whose names are on the slips. Instead, report income on the return of the individuals who contributed the funds to the account, in the proportion that the funds were supplied. For example, if only one spouse in a family works and is the source of all the deposits, then all the interest earned on the account is taxable to that person, no matter whose name is on the account.

- **Property transfers to a spouse.** A special rule applies when property is transferred to a spouse. Normally, such property transfers at tax cost, so that no gain or loss arises. This is true even if the spouse pays fair value for the property. The property will not transfer at tax cost, but at fair market value, provided the transferor files an election to have this happen with the tax return for the year of transfer and the spouse has paid fair value consideration.

- **Transfers for fair market consideration.** The Attribution Rules will not apply to any income, gain, or loss from transferred property if, at the time of transfer, consideration was paid for the equivalent of fair market value for the transferred property by the transferee. The person acquiring the property must use his or her own capital to pay for it.

- **Transfers for indebtedness.** The Attribution Rules on investment income will not apply if the transferee spouse borrowed capital from the transferor spouse, and the parties signed a bona fide loan that bore an interest rate, which is at least the lesser of:

   o the "prescribed" interest rates in effect at the time the indebtedness was incurred; and

   o the rate that would have been charged by a commercial lender.

Note that the prescribed interest rate used in establishing bona fide inter-spousal loans is set quarterly by the CRA. It is based on average yields of 90-day Treasury Bills for the first month of the preceding quarter. Interest must actually be paid on the indebtedness incurred by the spouse, under a formal loan agreement, by January 30 of each year, following the tax year, or attribution will apply to income earned with the loaned funds.

   o ***Second generation earnings.*** While the income earned on property transferred to the spouse must be reported by the transferor, any secondary income earned on investing the earnings is taxed in the hands of the transferee. This continues to be true for dividends sprinkled to non-active spouses from a private corporation.

o *Spousal dividend transfers.* One spouse may report dividends received from taxable Canadian corporations received by the other spouse if, by doing so, a Spousal Amount is created or increased. However, under Tax on Split Income (TOSI) below.

- **Assignment of Canada Pension Plan Benefits.** It is possible to apply (to Service Canada) to split CPP benefits between spouses, thereby minimizing tax on that income source in some cases. Both spouses must have reached age 60 to do so.

- **Pension income splitting.** The election to split up to 50% of eligible pension income between spouses does not involve the actual transfer of funds from one spouse to another, but is an election to have the split pension taxed as if it were the other spouse's income. It applies to qualifying sources, such as Registered Penson Plan benefits, which can be split at any age, or benefits from matured RRSPs or RRIFs, in which case, the recipient must be at least age 65. As such, the Attribution Rules do not apply. (However, if funds are actually transferred from one spouse to the other, the attribution rules will apply to any income earned on the transferred funds). Note also that if dividends are received from a private corporation, from a spouse that has reached at least age 65, 100% of those dividends may be reported by the spouse. More on that later.

FAMILY BUSINESS CONSIDERATIONS

Hiring Family Members. There are some special rules to observe when hiring family members, whether your business is incorporated or not. Family members can be hired as hourly employees, wage earners, sub-contractors, commission salespeople, or any other job that you would hire a stranger to do. You can pay them salary, wages, gratuities, overtime, premium hours, banked time, retroactive earnings, salary, bonuses, commissions, advances, draws, gifts, severance, sick leave, vacation pay, wages in lieu of notice, or a number of taxable or tax-free benefits.

However, a simple rule must be followed in hiring and remunerating your family members: *the process of hiring and paying your family member must be the same as that used to hire a non-related person, or in tax terms, that of a "non-arm's length" transaction.*

All of the appropriate paperwork must be in place, including the signing of employment contracts or sub-contracts, or the keeping of time cards to support hours worked. The appropriate T4 slips must be issued, and the payment must actually have been made to your family member, for work that was actually done. Equally important: the compensation paid must be no higher than what you would have paid to a stranger.

Without the appropriate paperwork and process, not only will it be impossible to write off the amounts paid to your family members, but you will also miss out on an important tax saver: the ability to legitimately split income from the business amongst family members, and to build important pension savings: through the Canada Pension Plan and by creating RRSP contribution room. You may also be in a position to pay your family members working in the business certain perks and benefits; some may be taxable, such as the benefit of driving a company-owned vehicle. Others may be tax free, such as the benefit of attaining educational qualifications that specifically benefit the employer.

It is always better to have the corporation pay for these expenses, because of its lower tax rates. Remember, however, that in order to deduct these expenses, they must be incurred for the purpose of earning income by the business.

Another issue that arises is whether you have an employer-employee relationship with your family members who work in your business. If they are employed by you, source deductions[9] must be deducted and remitted to the CRA on a periodic basis. CRA has issued guidance to assess the status of the people you engage, including family members. They are likely your employees if you take responsibility for the following areas:

- **Degree of Control.** The right to hire or fire, the timing and amount of compensation payments, the time, place where the work is done, and how it is done, including hours of work, training of human resources, client lists, territory to cover, and the assessment of the quality of work.

- **Ownership of Assets and Tools.** The purchase of equipment and tools required to do the work, including maintenance and repairs, insurance, rental, fuel, etc.

---

9 Source: CRA's publication RC4110 *Employed or Self-Employed*. Such deductions include income tax withholding, required Canada Pension Plan contributions, and employment insurance premiums if they qualify to receive EI Benefits.

- **Risk of Loss.** The assumption of the financial risk for the business undertakings and all operating costs.

- **Integration.** The fact that the business has multiple clients (as opposed to only one who controls the three factors above).

However, if the business is incorporated it may also be possible to pay family members other forms of remuneration; for example, dividends or capital gains, but only if new, strict guidelines are met. Otherwise "family income splitting" is thwarted, either by the Attribution Rules or the Tax on Split Income (TOSI) rules, described later.

Planning retirement income. If the active spouse in the family business corporation has reached age 65 in the year and dividends are distributed to the non-active spouse, the recipient spouse can avoid the punitive Tax on Split Income, which requires top rate taxes to be calculated on the first and all subsequent dollars distributed, and instead, claim progressive tax treatment on the dividends received. In fact, there is no limitation on how much income can be split, which is certainly very good news from a retirement planning point of view.

Recipient spouses will want to immediately invest unspent amounts in investment accounts in their own names to report subsequent investment earnings in their own right—a continued opportunity to receive tax-advantaged passive investment earnings on capital that originated in the business. The most tax-efficient investment to begin with is, of course, in a Tax Free Savings Account (TFSA).

Unfortunately, these more relaxed rules on splitting dividends with spouses in retirement do not provide a level playing field with employees, who get benefits from an employer-sponsored registered plan; those employees can income split at any age.

TOSI—Tax On Split Income. Since 1999, income sprinkled, generally by way of dividends, to minor children has invoked a "Kiddie Tax"; more formally known as a "Tax on Split Income". This requires calculations where progressive tax rates were applied, to a child's income, where this income was instead taxed at top marginal rates, from the first dollar so earned. This is calculated on Schedule 1 of the child's tax return, using form T1206.

Starting in 2018, such a Tax on Split Income (TOSI) applies to all adults, too, unless they fall into a specific exclusion, which contain three broad categories:

- Family members, *age 25 to 64*, who own shares that represent at *least 10% of the voting shares and value* of the company;

- Family members who are over age 17 who are "actively engaged" in the business; that is, if they averaged at least *20 hours per week* working in the business in the current year or in at least five previous years.

- Spouses of business owners *who are age 65 or older;*

The following are additional circumstances in which TOSI can be avoided:

- For anyone under 25 years old, income or gains from the disposition of property resulting from the *death of a parent* will be exempt. These family members will also escape TOSI if they are entitled to the *Disability Tax Credit* or are a *full-time student* in a post-secondary institution and received the money from someone *other than a parent.*

- Property transferred, at any age, due to a separation agreement or judgement due to *marriage or common-law relationship breakdowns.*

- Taxable capital gains resulting from deemed disposition on *death of a taxpayer.*

- Taxable capital gains resulting from dispositions of *qualified farm or fishing enterprises or qualifying small business corporation shares.*

- Income received by a spouse or common-law partner from the *active spouse who has reached age 65,* or in cases where the amounts were received as a result of the source spouse's death.

Note that for the purposes of these exclusions, related individuals for these purposes does not include aunts, uncles, nieces, or nephews.

New Definitions—Family Income Splitting: As you discuss these new rules with your tax advisor, you may find a number of new definitions are disclosed:

Specified Individuals. The recipient of the money from the private corporation is called the *"specified individual."* This is generally an adult resident in Canada. Note that non-residents, in general, will not be caught by the rules. Neither will adult residents who earn split income from "Excluded Businesses", described more fully below. Special rules will apply for family members who are 18 to 24 years old.

Source Individuals. This is the active participant in the business and/or shareholder who is related to the specified individual.

Split Income. The definition of *Split Income* includes the following amounts received from *any* "related business" carried on by a *"source individual"*:

- Taxable dividends from a private corporation

- Shareholder benefits

- Partnership, corporation, or trust income earned by a source individual in any related business or a source individual who has an interest—directly or indirectly—in any such organizations.

- Rental income from a property owned by a source individual

- Income from the indebtedness in a corporation, partnership, or trust (Note that debt obligations from mutual fund corporations or corporation shares of a class of the capital stock listed on a designated stock exchange are excluded.)

- Income or gains from the disposition of any of the properties above, including a taxable capital gain or a profit from the disposition of property after 2017.

Note that a *"related business"* is one in which the source individual owns shares of the capital stock of the corporation or property that derives all or part of its *fair market value* from the shares of the capital stock of the corporation, either directly or indirectly, at any time of the year.

Excluded Business. This is an important definition that describes the tax treatment of income received by those who make a *labor or capital contribution* to the private corporation in exchange for a reasonable return. In general, there are two ways for specified individuals to avoid paying top marginal rates on distributions from a private corporation:

> *General Exclusion:* Adult family members who are residents of Canada and who are "actively engaged" on a "regular, continuous, and substantial basis" in the private corporation during the tax year or *any five years at any time in the past*, will escape the punitive top-rate taxes.

> *"Actively engaged"* will require a *labor contribution* of at least 20 hours per week during the portion of the year in which a business operates. This rule recognizes the unique circumstances of seasonal businesses, such as farming or income tax preparation.

Capital contributions. If not actively engaged, as described above, the specified individual will need to meet more onerous criteria to avoid the top marginal tax rates on income or capital distributions. This will break down into whether the income comes from *Excluded Shares* or from capital contributions subject to specific rules described below.

Excluded Shares. In the following cases, the income received by the specified individual *will not* be subject to TOSI:

- If less than 90% of the income or gains received relate to a service business
- If the private corporation is not a professional corporation
- If the recipient of the income or gains owns shares that are equal to at least 10% of the voting shares and 10% of the value of the shares and
- Less than 10% of the income in the last year was from another related business

Capital Contributions. For those between the ages of 18 and 24 who loan money to the family business, *income earned on capital contributed may be subject to TOSI.*

To avoid TOSI, two tests may be applied. The first is based on a "Safe Harbour Capital Return"; the second is a reasonableness test based on *"Arm's Length Capital."*

If the amount paid to the specified individual on capital contributed is within the *Safe Harbor Capital Return*, it is is possible to reduce income subject to TOSI by a notional amount that multiplies the FMV of the property contributed by the prescribed rate of interest. Only this amount is considered to be "reasonable" and as a result, the amounts are taxed under the regular tax system and its progressive tax rates. Amounts paid above this formula will be subject to TOSI rules and top tax rates.

The return on the investment of *Arm's Length Capital* made by these individuals will not be subject to TOSI as long as the capital itself was not borrowed, or earned from property that was transferred or received from a related person, and the return earned was reasonable. Specifically, the property must not have been:

- Acquired as income, profit, or taxable capital gains from the disposition of a related business of the specified individual
- Borrowed by under a loan or other indebtedness

- Transferred, directly or indirectly, by any means, by a related individual, other than as a consequence of death.

CRA will take relevant factors into account in determining whether income will be subject to TOSI. The better your documentation on the labor or capital contributions made by your family members, the better you'll be able to face these audit tests. Under usual record retention rules, records are required no longer than 6 years after the date on the Notice of Assessment or Reassessment. These new rules will require that you keep lengthy and detailed records throughout the entire time your family member contributed to the business, as described below.

MANAGING MORE SOLUTIONS

The audit tests that must be met when family members work in a business, whether unincorporated or in a private corporation, are particularly onerous and will come under increasing scrutiny over the coming years. If you are hiring family members in the business, be sure to:

- *Identify the status of your human resources properly*—if employed by you, be sure to have an employment contract with proper role description attached, pay according to the same scales you would offer to a stranger, make sure the money is actually paid, and that source deductions are properly remitted together with required T4 Slips. If you are employing family members who are subcontractors, be sure that they, rather than you, meet the four criteria outlined by CRA that determines self employment: control, acquisition of tools and equipment, risk assumption, and integration of performance with several clients.

- *Observe the Attribution Rules*—it is not possible to transfer or loan funds for the purposes of income splitting to spouses or minor children, except in specific circumstances. The transferor will be required to report the income if the exceptions don't apply.

- *Understand the new TOSI requirements.*

To the latter point, specified individuals, those potentially subject to Tax on Split Income received from a privately held corporation, must be prepared to show that they have earned a "reasonable return" by meeting the "Reasonableness Criteria" administered by CRA. What's particularly important to note here is that the onus of proof has, in fact, been transferred to the taxpayer who receives the split income.

Four types of contributions will be reviewed on a tax audit. Discuss these with your tax specialist so that you can be sure to keep the required documentation at hand. Here are guidelines from the CRA:

- **A Labor Contribution.** CRA will pass judgement on the following:

  o The nature of the tasks performed; hours required to complete the tasks

  o What a competitive salary/wage is for roles in similar businesses in the marketplace

  o Time spent on the activities and the nature of the activities

  o The individual's education, training, experience, knowledge, skills, and know-how, as well as past performance of the functions

- **Property Contributions.** Here, CRA will look at the following:

  o Details on amounts of capital contributed to the business and amounts of loans

  o FMV of tangible and intangible property transferred (including technical knowledge experience, skill, or know-how)

  o Whether other sources of capital or loans were readily available

  o Whether comparable property was readily available

  o Whether property was unique or personal to the individual

  o "Opportunity costs" and past property contributions.

- **Risk Assumption.** This will include:

  o The degree to which the individual is exposed to the financial risks of the liabilities of the company, including statutory liabilities

  o The extent to which the contributions might be lost

  o Whether the risk is indemnified, and

  o Whether the individual's reputation or personal goodwill is at risk (how to justify this is a still a bit of a mystery). In addition, past or ongoing risk assumption will be considered.

- **Total Amounts Paid.** To determine if amounts paid to a family member are reasonable, taxpayers will need to look into the past: all other amounts "previously paid," including salary or other remuneration, dividends, interest, proceeds, and fees, as well as benefits and deemed payments will be considered. Clearly, in all cases, family members must be prepared to provide lengthy and detailed logs of their unique intellectual and financial contributions throughout the business lifecycle.

New Rules on the Acquisition of Depreciable Assets. Canada's competitive advantage in the global economy has been of concern since corporate tax reforms were introduced, both in the United States and in Canada. In the November 21, 2018 Fall Economic Update, new provisions were introduced to encourage businesses to invest in equipment. Several proposed changes were made to the allowable claims for Capital Cost Allowance (CCA) on assets acquired after November 20, 2018, and before 2028. (There was little by way of support, however, for new economy solutions, such as incentives to develop knowledge-based capital.)

That's a missed opportunity as many countries are now investing significant resources into the development of intellectual property rights; comparable to what they're putting into physical capital, such as machinery, equipment and buildings." In a 2013 report entitled *"Supporting Investment in Knowledge Capital, Growth and Innovation"*, the OECD notes "New thinking is needed to update a range of policy frameworks—from tax and competition policies to corporate reporting and intellectual property rights."

Following is a synopsis of the recent changes to the write-offs available for tangible assets:

For most capital assets—except class 53: manufacturing and processing machinery and equipment, and classes 43.1 and 43.2: clean energy equipment:

- First-year claims for deductions will be tripled for purchases between November 20, 2018, and December 32, 2023.

- Rather than restricting the claim to 50% of the normal Capital Cost Allowance (CCA) claim (half-year rule), the claim will be 150% of the normal CCA deduction.

- For purchases in years 2024 to 2027, the half-year rule will be suspended and where the half-year rule does not apply, the claim will be 125% of the normal claim.

- For purchase after 2027, the current rules will apply.

For class 53—manufacturing and processing machinery and equipment:

- The CCA rate will be 100 % for purchases between November 20, 2018, and the end of 2023.

- For purchases in 2024 and 2025, the rate will be 75%

- For purchases in 2026 and 2027, the rate will be 55%.

- For purchases after 2027, the rate will return to 30% subject to the half-year rule.

For class 43.1 and 43.2—clean energy equipment, the same rules for class 53 will apply for purchases between November 20, 2018, and December 31, 2027. After that, the current rules will apply.

In each case, the additional first-year claim will not affect the total amount of CCA that may be claimed in respect of any asset. As is currently the case, when assets are disposed of for more than their undepreciated capital cost, the excess claims will have to be recaptured. One exception is class 10.1 (passenger vehicles that cost more than $30,000).

New Rules for the Taxation of Active and Passive Income

Saving money inside a private corporation is important for several reasons: it shores up operating lines and the opportunity to borrow for business growth. It provides a financial safety net, should business plans faulter with Black Swan events. But, against these risk factors, there is an advantage: investing within a corporation allows for the deposit of bigger dollars—and therefore, a growth boost—as corporate tax rates are lower than those that are charged to individuals.

To reduce this advantage, the federal government has raised taxes for companies with significant investments within their private corporations, starting January 1, 2019, based on the amount of passive income earned in the prior year.

Specifically, the Small Business Deduction (SBD) will be "clawed back" when passive investment earnings in a private corporation exceed $50,000. However, this change is also accompanied by a reduction in the small business tax rate, which in turn, affects the rate of taxation that is applied when dividends are distributed into personal hands. These changes are discussed below:

Changes to the Small Business Tax Rate. When Active Business Income (ABI) eligible for the $500,000 Small Business Deduction (SBD) is earned, tax rates will be reduced to 9% for 2019 and future years.

Dividend Tax Credit Changes. Dividends paid out of the retained earnings of private corporations are classified into two categories:

- "Eligible dividends" originate from active business income earned above the small business deduction, which is taxed at the general rate of 15%. This includes any eligible portfolio dividends.

- "Non-eligible dividends" stem from active income taxed at the low small business tax rates and any passive investment income earned in the corporation (however, this excludes eligible portfolio dividends and the non-taxable portion of capital gains, which may be distributed as tax-free capital dividends.)

The calculation of the tax on non-eligible dividends that are distributed into personal hands of the shareholders will change, as a result of the reduction in the small business tax rate. A brief history of the calculations follows:

Year	Small Business Tax Rate	Dividend Gross Up Rate	Dividend Tax Credit Rate*	Dividend Tax Credit Rate**
2015	11.0%	18%	11.0%	13/18
2016	10.5%	17%	10.5%	21/29
2017	10.5%	17%	10.5%	21/29
2018	10.0%	16%	10.03%	8/11
2019	9.0%	15%	9.03%	9/13

*as a percentage of the grossed-up dividend   ** as a fraction of the gross-up

Reduction of the Small Business Deduction. The Small Business Deduction, which is also known as the business limit, is reduced on a *straight-line basis* when there is between $10 Million and $15 Million of taxable capital employed in Canada. The Small Business Deduction is not allowed when taxable capital exceeds $15 Million.

Now, for tax years after 2018, private corporations that earn more than $150,000 in passive investment income that is not incidental to an active business will pay tax on their active income at the general tax rate, currently 15%. If both restrictions apply to the corporation, the greater of the two will apply.

More specifically, the business limit of $500,000 will be reduced, also on a straight-line basis, when Canadian Controlled Small Business Corporations (CCPCs) have passive investment income between $50,000 and $150,000. The reduction in the business limit is calculated as $5 for every $1 of "adjusted aggregate investment income" above $50,000 and will be calculated annually *based on the prior year's passive investment income*. This will allow for some investment planning with your tax specialists.

The new tax calculations focus on three things: (i) the *Adjusted Aggregate Investment Income*; (ii) the small business deduction available; and (iii) the amount of active business income earned. The calculation of the *Adjusted Aggregate Investment Income* used for these purposes will not include:

- Taxable capital gains and losses on the disposition of property used principally in an active business, carried on primarily (50% or more) in Canada, by the CCPC or a related CCPC;

- The disposition of a share of another connected CCPC, where all or substantially all of the fair market value of the assets is used primarily in Canada in an active business of the CCPC; and

- Net capital losses carried over from other tax years.

But, the following sources **must be** included in the calculation:

- Dividends from non-connected corporations; and

- Income from savings in a non-exempt life insurance policy, if it is not otherwise included in the Adjusted Aggregate Investment Income.

Disposition of Qualifying Corporations. Remember that when it comes to taxable capital gains from the disposition of qualified farm or fishing property or qualified small business corporation shares, the amounts will be excluded from the split-income calculations, if the individual is over the age of 17 years or if the capital gain arises, at any age, from the death of an individual, or if the amounts arise pursuant to a court order or written separation agreement. This brings a huge advantage to the family: the distribution of a tax-free gain on the disposition of the family business shares, often in the millions of dollars.

However, for those ***under the age of 18 years***, twice the amount of taxable capital gains from the disposition of private corporation shares will attract an income inclusion of a non-eligible dividend, subject to tax at the highest marginal tax rates.

Lifetime Capital Gains Exemption (LCGE). When a company qualifies for a special provision, the Lifetime Capital Gains Exemption (LCGE), it is possible to exponentially increase the after-tax value in the family business. This deduction, available since 1985, was originally a $500,000 amount (but reduced to $100,000 for most property in 1988), and was available to each individual over a lifetime, on net capital gains realized on the disposition of any capital asset.

Over the years, the provisions have changed significantly. Notably, it was limited to three specific types of assets as of February 22, 1994: qualified farm or fishing property, and qualifying small business corporation shares. In the April 21, 2015 Federal Budget, this deduction was expanded to $1 Million on the disposition of qualified farm or fishing property disposed of after April 20, 2015, and for dispositions of qualified small business corporation shares, an indexed lifetime exemption at recent thresholds shown below:

Lifetime Capital Gains Exemption

For qualified farm or fishing property and qualified small business corporation shares

Year	2019	2018	2017	2016
Exemption limit	$866,912	$848,252	$835,716	$824,176
Deduction limit (½ of the capital gain is taxable)	433,456	424,126	417,858	412,088
Additional exemption amount for qualified farm or fishing property	133,088	151,748	164,284	175,824
Additional deduction amount for qualified farm or fishing property (½ of the capital gain is taxable)	66,544	75,874	82,142	87,912

Source: CRA Website

Eligibility. For the shares to qualify, a business needs to meet the following criteria:

1. The corporation must be a Canadian-controlled Private Corporate, in which 90% or more of the FMV of the assets are mainly used in an active business carried on 50% of the time or more in Canada by the corporation, a related corporation, or a connected corporation. Proprietorships or unincorporated businesses do not qualify.

2. All of the following conditions must also apply:

   a. At the time of sale, the shares sold were owned by the taxpayer, his/her spouse or common-law partner, or a partnership in which the owner was a member.

b. In the 24 months immediately before the disposition, more than 50% of the FMV assets were used in an active business carried on primarily in Canada, and no one other than you, *a person related to you*, or a partnership of which you were a member owned the shares.

c. If shares were issued after June 13, 1988, it is considered that immediately before the shares were issued, they were owned by an unrelated person (which means the 24 month holding period must be met). However, the rule won't apply in some instances, in which similar factors to the above can be established.

It is also important to note that some provisions will reduce or negate the Capital Gains Exemption, so ask your accountant to explain this area, so that you do not experience an expensive surprise on your Notice of Assessment in the year that your business is sold. It is necessary to track two numbers in computing the LCGE:

- The annual gains limit; and
- The cumulative gains limit.

The annual gains limit describes the net taxable capital gains for the current year that may qualify for the deduction (qualifying taxable capital gains of the year, including reserves and amounts that represent eligible capital property gains in 1988 and 1989), but this is reduced by:

- Current year allowable capital losses;
- Current year allowable business investment losses; and
- Net capital losses of other years applied in the current year.

If this number is a negative, the annual gains limit is nil and the LCGE is not available to you.

In addition, the cumulative gains limit describes the net amount of all gains that have qualified for the deduction since 1985. It is to this cumulative gains limit that the Cumulative Net Investment Loss (CNIL) calculation is applied. This is also a lifetime cumulative account, which compares the balance between your investment income and investment expenses. Net losses in the CNIL account after 1987 will reduce the LCGE.

Finally, the non-taxable part of the current year capital gains reported on the personal tax return could be subject to the Alternative Minimum Tax (AMT). While this tax is recoverable by applying it against taxes payable over the next seven years, it has the potential to be a nasty surprise, especially if you were expecting not to incur any taxes at all.

Special Rules for Acquiring Farmland or Fishing Property from Mom and Dad. The Income Tax Act allows for the transfer of farm property to a taxpayer's child at any amount between its cost and FMV. Therefore, the right choice of the amount of proceeds is one that maximizes the use of any LCGE available to the transferor to minimize the total taxes payable by the transferee later, without increasing the taxes to the transferor. Similar provisions are applicable to disposition of qualified fishing property, effective May 2, 2006.

Considering Your Own Situation

At the time of writing, it is safe to say the risks to the taxation of value in a private corporation have not yet been fully put to bed by Finance Canada. Expect more changes. This does not represent the single biggest reason to start your retirement and estate planning as early in your lifetime as you can; but it is likely among the top three.

The first one, of course, is to ensure the health of your precious family relationships, well past your own demise. The second is to ensure that your spouse and family members—including the community if you so choose—keep at least as much as the CRA will. Be sure to work closely and stay in touch with your tax professionals, at least as part of your annual tax and estate planning activities.

In preparation for these discussions, consider the following areas:

- What are the most recent personal and corporate tax changes that affect my family and my business?

- Exactly how much more will these changes cost me, in terms of new corporate taxes?

- What will the cumulative family tax liability—the integration of the personal and corporate taxes owed by all of us—be this year, and projected into the future?

- What changes should be made to our investment strategy for capital held in the company?

- What effect will this new tax regime have on retirement savings?

- Is it still advantageous to save money inside the corporation, or should we plan to do so personally in the future?

Keep in mind that individual investors and unincorporated self-employed individuals who are outside of the corporation are affected by income splitting, too. There are several methods of family income splitting, discussed earlier, such as contributions to spousal RRSPs, the election to split eligible pension income from RPPs, matured RRSPs or RRIFs, drawing up inter-spousal loans or transfers to non-arm's length minor children, and the timing of the transfer of assets.

Contrary to initial proposals on corporate tax reforms, the integration of the personal/corporate tax system has been retained, with the preservation of three important provisions:

- The Capital Dividend Account, which allows for the tax free flow through of the exempt portion of capital gains into personal hands;

- The availability of the Lifetime Capital Gains Exemption, which can be designated out to beneficiaries of a discretionary family trust; and

- The recovery of the *Refundable Dividend Tax on Hand* (RDTOH), albeit with some timing differences for the reporting of non-eligible and eligible dividends.

In light of the various tax changes, it is important to meet with your tax accountant and address the following areas, in terms of your own situation:

- Does it still make sense to accumulate as much money in the corporate accounts?

- How should you structure retirement income from savings in the corporation?

- Should you change the timing of the realization of capital gains in your corporate investment accounts, by deferring disposition in order to preserve the small business deduction (that is, ensuring that passive investment income remains under $50,000)? You will also want to know how to maximize the use of capital losses to offset gains.

- Should you change your salary/dividend/bonus mix?

Depending on where you live, there might be advantages to averaging in more income to your family's hands personally, and instead, saving on a tax-deferred basis in an RRSP.

Complicated tax rules could thwart an otherwise "perfect" family financial plan: the transfer of assets from the higher earner to the lower earners in the family that would result in tax on income being paid at lower rates, leading to lower overall family taxes payable. However, what they do not do is strike out the most important aspect of our tax system: the legal right that Canadians have to arrange their affairs within the framework of the tax laws that are in place at the time, so as to only pay the correct amount of tax—as a family unit—and no more.

Make no mistake: a potential time bomb must be defused in order to protect the precious equity that has been built in a family business. Do it well and the stage is set to extinguish the exorbitant taxes payable that could arise, when tax saving opportunities are ignored. Also recognize that tax change will affect the transition of your business. Discuss potential tax risks that might arise with your professional advisory team.

It is vital to stay current on tax change to mitigate risks to your investment in the family business. Some excellent online resources, focused on the tax education needs of taxpayers and their advisors, include:

- **Knowledge Bureau Report.** Available at www.knowledgebureau. com.

- **EverGreen Explanatory Notes.** A sleek tax research library that provides easy-to-read educational information about personal, corporate, and GST/HST matters with the rights of the taxpayer in mind. Saving you precious time, it cuts and navigates through the thousands of pages in complicated publications and forms available from the CRA.

Index

A

accumulations, 26, 140

advisory fees, 79

agreements, legal documentation 94, 95, 99, 100-101, 105, 109-110, 143

alternative minimum tax, 146, 171

B

beneficial ownership 142

business advisor, 16, 34, 36, 48, 60, 89, 98, 104, 110-112, 114, 126, 145

business enterprise, 139, 155

business model, 8, 10, 13, 16, 25-30, 35, 41, 114

business plan 15, 17-20, 41, 85, 122, 133, 167

business transformation plan, 17, 18, 20, 23, 36

C

capital dividend account, 173

chartered business valuator, 105

crisis situations, 87, 89, 91, 93, 98, 100, 101

D

depreciable assets, 131, 166

dividend, 26, 45-46, 59

dividends 122, 125, 128, 129, 130, 132, 135, 136, 149, 150, 156, 158, 160, 167, 168

dividend tax credit, 168

due diligence, 104, 110, 113, 114

H

holdco-opco, 148

holding company, 26, 137, 150

human resources, see employees

I

income splitting, 129, 132, 135, 141, 149, 155, 158, 160, 161, 164, 173

integration, 81, 126, 160, 164, 172, 173

investment advisor, 24, 127

K

key person insurance, 95, 100

kiddie tax, 160

L

leverage, 111, 112

lifestyle family business, 14, 16-18, 20, 22, 23, 38, 40, 44 47, 49, 57, 79, 89, 90, 97

lifetime capital gains exemption, 130, 141, 142, 170-172

long term planning, 125, 126, 145

M

market driven business, 12-23, 40, 47, 49-50, 53, 57, 61, 64, 69, 75, 76, 79, 82, 91

marketplace opportunities, 10, 23

merger, 92, 94, 104, 106, 108, 111-113, 120, 121, 141, 145

multi-stakeholder, 123, 125, 126, 127, 130, 132, 143, 152

ABOUT THE AUTHORS

Jenifer Bartman, CPA, CA, CMC, MFA is the Founder & Principal of Jenifer Bartman Business Advisory Services, assisting companies in transition (early, financing, growth, and succession stages) with growth strategies, financing readiness, strategic/business planning, and executive coaching. Jenifer is well known for her venture capital and early stage financing expertise, having been an executive in the industry and an advisor to many young companies. She appears on the CBC News Network Weekend Business Panel. Follow her on twitter @JeniferInc.

Evelyn Jacks, MFA, DFA-Tax Services Specialist is one of Canada's most prolific financial authors, having penned 53 books on personal tax and family wealth management, many of them best-sellers. A well known tax and financial commentator, she has twice been named one of Canada's Top 25 Women of Influence. Evelyn is also President of Knowledge Bureau, a national educational institute focused on professional development of tax and financial advisors. Follow her on twitter @evelynjacks and in Knowledge Bureau Report.